EXCAVATIONS

IN THE

TOMBS OF THE KINGS.

ENTRANCE TO THE TOMB OF HARMHABI.

THEODORE M. DAVIS'
EXCAVATIONS: BIBÂN EL MOLÛK

THE TOMBS OF HARMHABI

AND

TOUATÂNKHAMANOU

THE DISCOVERY OF THE TOMBS

BY

THEODORE M. DAVIS

KING HARMHABI AND TOUATÂNKHAMANOU

BY

SIR GASTON MASPERO

CATALOGUE OF THE OBJECTS DISCOVERED

BY

GEORGE DARESSY

ILLUSTRATIONS

BY

LANCELOT CRANE

Duckworth

First published in 1912
by Archibald Constable & Co. Ltd.
Reprinted in 2001 by
Gerald Duckworth & Co. Ltd.
61 Frith Street, London W1D 3JL
Tel: 020 7434 4242
Fax: 020 7434 4420
Email: enquiries@duckworth-publishers.co.uk
www.ducknet.co.uk

Foreword © 2001 by Nicholas Reeves

A catalogue record for this book is available
from the British Library

ISBN 0 7156 3072 5

Printed in Great Britain by Bath Press, Bath

FOREWORD

'Wriggling and crawling, we pushed and pulled ourselves down the sloping rubbish, until, with a rattling avalanche of small stones, we arrived at the bottom of the passage, where we scrambled to our feet at the brink of a large rectangular well, or shaft. Holding the lamps aloft, the surrounding walls were seen to be covered with wonderfully preserved paintings …; [while] through the window-like aperture [ahead], a dim suggestion could be obtained of a white-pillared hall. The intense eagerness to know what was beyond, and, at the same time, the feeling that it was almost desecration to climb into those halls which had stood silent for thousands of years, cast a spell over the scene and made it unforgettable.'

(Arthur Weigall, *The Glory of the Pharaohs*,
London, 1923, pp. 167-8)

The tomb of pharaoh Horemheb [Harmhabi], founder of the 19th Dynasty, was brought to light on 22 February 1908, some thirty centuries after it had finally been closed by the priests and necropolis workmen of the 21st Dynasty. The discoverer was a wealthy American enthusiast by the name of Theodore M. Davis, his find the latest in a string of archaeological triumphs chalked up in the Valley of the Kings since 1902. Preliminary investigation revealed a series of rock-cut staircases pushing deep into the ground to give access to a burial suite of more than a dozen rooms. Here, within these chambers, Tutankhamun's one-time general, unexpectedly elevated from commoner to king, had been interred; and here, in death, Horemheb's being would merge with the sun-god as it was reborn each and every day.

Pharaoh's tomb had been plundered in antiquity by robbers and the State, and scattered throughout the rubble fill were tantalising remnants of its original, once-splendid burial furniture. Here, too, was a superbly crafted sarcophagus, and an intriguing collection of bones – the remains, doubtless, of the king himself and perhaps other royals, gathered up from around the Valley for safe reburial during and after the closing years of the New Kingdom. But the real treasure was on the walls – some of the finest painted reliefs to have survived from antiquity (for which the reader is referred to E. Hornung, *Das Grab des Haremhab im Tal der Könige* [Bern, 1971]), in various stages of production, intact and reflecting still a wealth of brilliant colour in the light of the explorers' trembling torches.

Davis's publication of his discovery – *The Tombs of Harmhabi and Touatânkhamanou* – proved his swan-song, appearing in 1912 just three years before his death. A classic of Egyptian archaeology and a work of fundamental importance, it contains the only account of the tomb's excavation and finds ever published. The book is illustrated by a series of splendid watercolours by Lancelot Crane (son of the artist Walter Crane), and an important and comprehensive collection, by Harry Burton, of some of the most evocative photographs of the royal burial-ground ever taken – the Valley of the Kings at the height of its romantic splendour.

What of the other tomb in the title? Theodore Davis's report is home to a remark which, had he lived, would have come back cruelly to haunt him: 'I fear that the Valley of the Tombs is now exhausted.' A mere ten years later, Howard Carter and Lord Carnarvon, digging further down the Valley, would reveal to a startled world a burial Davis imagined, mistakenly, he had already found. It was the magnificent, virtually intact tomb of Tutankhamun – 'Touatânkhamanou'.

London, January 2001   Nicholas Reeves

CONTENTS.

LIST OF ILLUSTRATIONS.

PLAN.

I.

THE FINDING OF THE TOMBS OF HARMHABI AND TOUATÂNKHAMANOU.

By THEODORE M. DAVIS.

On the 25th of February, 1908, while working in the Valley of the Tombs of the Kings, we came upon signs of a tomb, and, after a day's work, discovered a stairway leading sharply down a few feet, where broken rock and sand filled the space almost to the top. It was impossible to advance except by digging our way with our hands—and, as we were most anxious to find whose tomb it was, my assistant, Mr. Ayrton, in spite of the heat, undertook the difficult task of crawling over the sharp rocks and sand on his hands and feet for some distance, when to the astonishment of all of us, he found on the sides of the wall a hieratic inscription, containing the name of Harmhabi.

This was a surprise, as we had always thought that Harmhabi was buried at Memphis, or at some place in Lower Egypt. On the 29th of February I made my way down into the tomb with Mr. Ayrton and three others. It was necessary to drag ourselves over the stones and sand which blocked the way, with our heads unpleasantly near the rough roof; there was little air, except that which came from the mouth of the tomb 130 feet above, and the heat was stifling. The sand over which we had passed had evidently been put there for the protection of the body of Harmhabi. Beyond the sand, we came to an open well or pit, cut vertically in the rock; this was for the purpose of receiving any water which might find its way from the mouth of the tomb, and to aid the discharge of the water a smaller room had been cut in the rock next the well. We crossed this well by using a ladder which landed us on the rock above.

And, just here, it may be interesting to explain how the robbers got into and out of the well, and then continued their way to the end of the tomb.

A few years ago, in entering the tomb of Thoutmôsis IV, we found a rope tied to a column, by which they let themselves down to the level of the well, and in some way threw a loop rope over a large rock above, on the other side of this well, and so pulled themselves up to the level above. This rope remains in its original place.

Above this well in the tomb of Harmhabi the walls on three sides were covered with paintings, but the one opposite to the entrance to this pit had been partially destroyed, showing that the robbers in both instances had not been deceived by the painted wall, but had broken through the concealed entrance and found their way to the funeral chambers, ruthlessly destroying their beautiful and valuable contents. After gaining this broken entrance we made our way for 180 feet to the bottom of the tomb. The walls of this corridor were adorned with paintings of the king and the gods—many of them unfinished. At the lowest point of the tomb, in a room about ten feet square, is a remarkable painting of Osiris on stone—somewhat larger than life—and quite unique.

The last and largest room contained the sarcophagus of Harmhabi, made of red granite—8 feet 11 inches in length, 3 feet 9½ inches wide, and 4 feet in height—in perfect condition, and one of the most beautiful ever found. Also in this room were many interesting objects—a germinating form of Osiris, described in the Catalogue, and a number of small gods, 10 inches high, made of wood and painted black, which surrounded the sarcophagus.

In the Osiris room there were the bones of two women found. In the room of the sarcophagus the skulls of two women and one man were lying on the floor, and in the sarcophagus there were the bones of one person. Dr. Elliot Smith kindly examined these bones, and named them, but could not decide upon the gender of those in the sarcophagus.

In the winter of 1906, while digging near the foot of a high hill in the Valley of the Tombs of the Kings, my attention was attracted to a large rock tilted to one side, and for some mysterious reason I felt interested in it, and on being carefully examined and dug about by my assistant, Mr. Ayrton, with the hands, the beautiful blue cup described in Mr. Daressy's catalogue was found. This bore the cartouche of Touatânkhamanou. The following year, in digging to the north of Harmhabi's tomb, we came upon signs of another, and my assistant, Mr. E. Harold Jones, put his men to work, and at the depth of 25 feet we found a room filled almost to the top with dried mud, showing that water had entered it. And it was curious to see the decorative manner in which the mud had dried.

We found a broken box containing several pieces of gold leaf stamped with the names of Touatânkhamanou and his wife Ankhousnamanou—also the names Divine Father Aîya and his wife Tîyi, but without title or prenomen. We also found under the mud, lying on the floor in one corner, the beautiful alabaster statuette described in Mr. Daressy's catalogue. A few days after this we came upon a pit, some distance from the tomb, filled with large earthen pots containing what would seem to be the débris from a tomb, such as dried wreaths of leaves and flowers, and small bags containing a powdered substance. The cover of one of these jars had been broken, and wrapped about it was a cloth on which was inscribed the name of Touatânkhamanou.

The finding of the blue cup with the cartouche of Touatânkhamanou, and not far from it the quite undecorated tomb containing the gold leaf inscribed with the names of Touatânkhamanou and Ankhousnamanou, in connection with the Divine Father Aîya and his wife Tîyi, and the pit containing the jars with the name of Touatânkhamanou, lead me to conclude that Touatânkhamanou was originally buried in the tomb described above, and that it was afterwards robbed, leaving the few things that I have mentioned.

I fear that the Valley of the Tombs is now exhausted. I began my work of exploration in 1903, and between that date and 1909, I found seven important inscribed tombs—those of Thoutmôsis IV—Hatshopsouîtou—Iouiya and Touiyou—Siphtah—Prince Mentuherkhepshef—Tîyi—and Harmhabi —also nine uninscribed tombs, one of them containing the beautiful gold jewellery of Setuî II and Taouasrît, one with pieces of gold leaf with the names of Touatânkhamanou and Aîya, and a small alabaster figure.

My thanks are due to Sir Gaston Maspero for his important Life of Harmhabi, to Monsieur Daressy for his admirable descriptive catalogue, and to Mr. Edward Ayrton for his faithful work in opening and clearing the tomb. He has written an exhaustive report which, owing to the size of this volume, I am unable to include, but which he is at liberty to use as he thinks best. Also to Mr. Lancelot Crane for his artistic copies of the paintings in the tomb, done under most difficult conditions.

LUXOR, *February* 16, 1912.

II.

NOTE ON
THE LIFE AND MONUMENTS OF HARMHABI.

BY SIR GASTON MASPERO.

THE reign of Harmhabi marks one of the turning-points in the history of Egypt. Coming as he did after the heretic Pharaohs, Harmhabi gave the final victory to the priests of Amon and established the supremacy of the sacerdotal over the warlike spirit. After him, Egypt had other conquering rulers who attempted to maintain or restore her domination over Asia, but these sovereigns, more and more bound and weighed down by religious practices, knew not how to preserve their independence against the colleges of priests. Thebes, which had given the land its most warlike dynasties, gradually became the mere appanage of a god; governed by the priests or priestesses of Amon, the city which had been originally a military kingdom became gradually the seat of a veritable theocracy. There is, therefore, real interest in the close study of the monuments of the Pharaoh under whom it would seem that this transformation began actually to take place.

§ I.—NAMES, ORIGIN, AND FAMILY OF HARMHABI.

The complete protocol of the Pharaoh Harmhabi is rarely to be found on monuments. In its most developed form it goes thus :[1]

[1] Lepsius, *Königsbuch*, Pl. XXX, No. 410; Bouriant–Brugsch, *Le Livre des Rois*, pp. 56–57.

The variations of the name of Horus are purely graphic ⟨hieroglyphs⟩ for ⟨hieroglyphs⟩, as are those of the *Nabuît*-name ⟨hieroglyph⟩; and those of the Golden Horus are partly graphic, ⟨hieroglyph⟩ for ⟨hieroglyph⟩, but they also involve some modifications in the accepted text such as ⟨hieroglyphs⟩.[1] The cartouches vary still more. Some of them only contain the fundamental forms ⟨cartouche⟩, ⟨cartouche⟩, ⟨cartouche⟩, ⟨cartouche⟩; in others those forms are enlarged sometimes by the addition of epithets, at least where the first cartouche is concerned ⟨cartouche⟩, ⟨cartouche⟩, ⟨cartouche⟩.[2] Champollion deciphered the name, at first, as Hôr-nem-neb,[3] and then correctly enough as Horhemhbai, but, neglecting the adventitious elements which figure in it, he thought he could read in the first ⟨hieroglyph⟩ or ⟨hieroglyph⟩ the origin of the name ῏Ωρος—Horus, which is to be met with in the Lists of Manetho[4] coupled with a reign of thirty-five or forty years. Devéria[5] showed subsequently that the Greek transcription of the Egyptian name is *Armais*, and since his time no serious objection has been raised to his demonstration. The Egyptian ⟨hieroglyph⟩ was pronounced *v*, and easily became *w* in the Ramesside κοινή: the exact transcription into Greek of the name is therefore ᾽Αρμάϝις with a digamma which, subsequently dropped, became ᾽Αρμάϊς. In the name of the first Nectanebo the element ⟨hieroglyphs⟩ *Har-habi* is transcribed in the fourth century B.C. by -αῤῥάβης, according to the custom of the time. The transcription ᾽Αρμάϊς, which supposes the presence of the digamma, must date from a time when this letter was still in use. If that is really so, should we not consider that the legend which introduces Harmhabi into the story of Danaos is more ancient than has hitherto been supposed?

The names of the father and mother of Harmhabi are still unknown. As we shall see below,[6] he originally came from the city of ⟨hieroglyphs⟩ Hasuton, chief town of the XVIIIth Nome of Upper Egypt,[7] the ruins of which are probably hidden under one of the large Tells in the neighbourhood of Sheikh Fadl.

---

[1] Lepsius, *Königsbuch*, Pl. XXX, No. 410 *d*; Bouriant–Brugsch, *Le Livre des Rois*, p. 57.

[2] Lepsius, *Königsbuch*, Pl. XXX, No. 410 *g-i, l-m*; Bouriant–Brugsch, *Le Livre des Rois*, p. 57.

[3] Champollion, *Lettres à Mgr. le duc de Blacas*, vol. I, pp. 47 *sqq*.

[4] Unger, *Manetho*, pp. 157, 158.

[5] Devéria, *Œuvres Diverses*, vol. II, pp. 158–159, 162–163.

[6] See below, p. 11.

[7] Brugsch, *Dictionnaire Géographique*, pp. 669–671.

The terms of the inscription from which we learn this make it probable that he had been born hereditary ruler of this town, and consequently that his parents were princes of it before him. The text in which he affirms that he restored the edifices of Deir el-Baharî has sometimes been interpreted as a proof that he belonged to the line of the Ahmessides and, more exactly, that he was descended from Thoutmôsis III; the latter is here called ⟨hieroglyphs⟩ "the father of his fathers, Manakhpirrîya." The expression is too vague to entitle us to draw a definite conclusion from it. It agrees with the theory according to which the ancient Pharaoh, whose monuments the reigning Pharaoh repaired, was his blood-ancestor, "father of his fathers." It would be equally imprudent to deny or to affirm that Harmhabi was related by blood to the sovereigns of the XVIIIth Dynasty; the question must stand open until precise documents bring us a solution either in one sense or in another.

The wife of Harmhabi was one ⟨cartouche⟩ Nazmimaut,[1] who had the title of ⟨hieroglyphs⟩ "Royal Wife, Lady of Both Lands."[2] It has often been conjectured that she was a hereditary princess and that Harmhabi had, by marrying her, legalised the revolution which had brought him to the throne; some historians even supposed that an allusion to this marriage was to be found in the Turin inscription which reports his accession to the throne,[3] and others thought that that lady was identical with a certain ⟨hieroglyphs⟩ Nazmimaut, a sister of Queen Naftaiti, wife of Amenôthes IV.[4] Even if it had been the case it ought to have been admitted that such a marriage would not have provided Harmhabi with a very strong claim to the throne. Naftaiti herself does not appear to have belonged to the line of the Ahmessides, for she is called ⟨hieroglyphs⟩, ⟨hieroglyphs⟩, "Great Royal Wife," ⟨hieroglyphs⟩ "Great Royal Wife, Regent of the South and of the North, Lady of Both Lands,"[5] never ⟨hieroglyphs⟩ "Royal Daughter" or ⟨hieroglyphs⟩ "Royal Sister." Neither is Nazmimaut called the daughter or sister of a king on the monuments which

[1] Concerning the reading of this name, see Brugsch, *Thesaurus Inscriptionum Ægyptiacarum*, vol. V, p. 1074.

[2] Champollion, *Lettres à Mgr. le duc de Blacas*, vol. I, Pl. I; Lepsius, *Königsbuch*, Pl. XXX, No. 411. The Plate in Champollion's letter gives her title as ⟨hieroglyphs⟩ (Pl. II, No. 12), but this is a mere conjecture: the commentary states that the titles were lost in a fracture (p. 50).

[3] See below, p. 21.

[4] Bouriant–Brugsch, *Le Livre des Rois*, p. 55.

[5] Lepsius, *Königsbuch*, Pl. XXVII, Nos. 387, 389; Bouriant–Brugsch, *Le Livre des Rois*, pp 53, 54.

mention her, and the epithets [hieroglyphs] "Beloved of Isis the Divine Mother, Living for ever," which are given her on a Turin statue,[1] do not in any way enlighten us as to her origin. We must therefore, at any rate for the present, resign ourselves to remain in doubt as to who Queen Nazmimaut was by birth, and whether she brought to her husband a more or less authentic right to the crown.

Harmhabi is not known to have had either a son or a daughter.

§ II.—HARMHABI BEFORE HIS ACCESSION TO THE THRONE.

Some memory of his youth and of his administrative career has been preserved for us by two monuments : (1) an inscription engraved on the back of a black granite group, to be found in the Turin Museum, which represents Harmhabi seated on his throne, and Queen Nazmimaut standing by his side ;[2] (2) the fragments of his Memphis tomb, which are scattered among six museums or private collections.[3]

The inscription on the group, mentioned for the first time by Champollion,[4] was published *in extenso* in 1874 by Birch, after a copy by Bonomi,[5] and by Brugsch in 1891,[6] and, in part only, by Erman in 1904.[7] It has been translated into English by Birch[8] and by Breasted,[9] and into German by Brugsch.[10] It contains twenty-six lines, but the beginning of the first fourteen has disappeared for about one quarter of the whole length ; the lacunæ are not such as to prevent us from following the meaning. The part concerning the king's youth (lines 1–12) opens with the mutilated legend of Harmhabi [hieroglyphs] "beloved by the Horus of Hasute," then it goes on :

---

[1] Brugsch, *Thesaurus Inscriptionum Ægyptiacarum*, vol. V, p. 1073.

[2] Gazzera, *Descrizione del Museo Reale di Torino*, pp. 45, 46 ; Orcurti, *Catalogo Illustrato dei Monumenti Egizii*, vol. I, p. 60, No. 6. A drawing of this group is to be found in Rosellini's *Monumenti Reali*, Pl. LIV quinquies, A.

[3] Enumerated by Breasted, *King Harmhab and his Sakkara Tomb*, in the *Zeitschrift*, 1900 vol. XXXVIII, pp. 47, 50, and *Ancient Records of Egypt*, vol. III, pp. 4–12.

[4] Champollion, *Lettres à Mgr. le duc de Blacas*, vol. I, p. 48.

[5] Birch, *Inscription of Haremhebi on a Statue at Turin*, in the *Transactions of the Society oj Biblical Archæology*, vol. III, two plates facing pp. 486 and 487.

[6] H. Brugsch, *Thesaurus Inscriptionum Ægyptiacarum*, vol. V, pp. 1073–1078.

[7] A. Erman, *Ægyptische Chrestomathie*, pp. 102–106 and 51*–53*.

[8] Birch, *Inscription of King Haremhebi*, in the *Transactions*, vol. III, pp. 491–495 ; and *Records of the Past*, 1st sec., vol. X, pp. 29–36.

[9] Breasted, *Ancient Records of Egypt*, vol. III, pp. 14–19.

[10] H. Brugsch, *Geschichte Ægyptens*, pp. 440–444.

[hieroglyphic text spanning the upper portion of the page]

Already before his birth "Amonrâsonthêr nourished him, Harsiesi was his
    "safeguard by the charms he made for his limbs.   He came forth from
    "the womb clothed in strength, with the complexion of a god on him,

---

[1] The lacunæ in this place represent about one-fourth of the total line.
[2] In the original the woman who nurses the child is represented sitting on a chair.

"and he did . . . . Shoulders were lowered before him when he
"was still a nurseling, and great and small went down on their faces,
"hastening to bring victuals and provisions.   When he was still a child
"without reason . . . . for the whole people, and there was
"apparent a divine emanation in his complexion for whoever gazed on
"his form, to wit, the strength of his father Horus ; for he (Horus) had
"placed himself before him, having created him, in order to enact his
"protection towards him, and the corporation brought everything . . . . . .
"He knew the day in which to unite with him to give him his kingship.
"Now behold, this god held his son up[1] in the sight of the whole people
"because he wished to enlarge his course of life until the day should
"come when he would assume his (kingly) dignity.   He therefore gave
"(him) . . . . of his time.   The king's heart was satisfied with
"his talents, and glad to choose him, he made him the Supreme Chief
"of the land, to make fast the laws of both countries,[2] the Prince of this
"land in its entirety, so that he was a unique Person without a second ;
"(of whom) the designs . . . . . . (he pleased) the whole people by what
"issued from his mouth.   When he was called to the presence of the
"Sovereign because the palace had fallen into trouble, as soon as he
"opened his mouth and answered the King, he soothed him by what
"issued from his mouth, for he alone was excellent, without (a second)
". . . . . ., all his designs were as the steps of the Ibis,[3] his decisions
"were the emanations of the Master of Hasrô,[4] jubilant for that which
"is straight as Fondi,[5] rejoicing in his heart like Phtah,[6] when he awoke
"in the morning he made his offering of it[7] . . . . (for he who

[1] Literally, "*separated* his son."

[2] Literally, "he established him supreme chief of the land, that he may land the laws of both countries."   I find no modern expression rendering the metaphor in the Egyptian ⬚⬚, to land, to make a boat fast to the bank of the river.

[3] This metaphor means, generally speaking, that Harmhabi's designs progressed as those of Thot himself.

[4] The Master of Hasrô here means Thot ; elsewhere this appellation is applied to Osiris.

[5] ⬚ Fondi, Fonti, in the Memphitic period ⬚ Fonzi, lit.: "*Naso*, the long-nosed god," an epithet which Thot the Ibis owed to his long beak.

[6] Phtah is ⬚ "master of that which is straight," and he is raised on the cubit ⬚, which explains why he should here be mentioned by the side of Thot.

[7] "It" means here ⬚ "that which is straight."   It is probably an allusion to the moment in the religious service when the king offered the gods an image of ⬚ Maâit—Truth and Justice—as a proof that he was straightforward in his devotion to them and true to his people.

" rules by Truth) his talents and who walks in its ways, it protects him
" on earth for the length of eternity. — Now behold, while he governed
" both lands over a spell of many years, (the officers of the State brought
" unto him) every matter ; the councillors (came) to (him), with bent
" backs, at the outer door of the Palace ; the chiefs of the Barbarians,
" from the South as from the North, ran up to him, their hands stretched
" out to him, they praised him to his face like unto a god, and all that
" was done was done by his orders . . . . As he went on, the fear
" which he inspired grew in the face of the whole people, they prayed
" that he should have health and strength,[1] they acclaimed in him ' the
" Father of both lands, the enlightened Reason which the god had given
" as a landing-place for the laws of both countries.[2] ' "

A few general data, sufficiently probable to be admitted into history, may
be extracted from this somewhat commonplace phraseology. First, the
indication, as Harmhabi's birthplace, of the town ⌷ ⥯ ◠ or, in inverted terms,
⥯ ◠ ⌷.[3] Its god, Horus, extended over " his son " the same protection that
other gods extended over noble families in their localities. The terms used
by the scribe who wrote the text lead us to suppose that, after inheriting
feudal power from his parents and exercising it for some time, he left his
lands and went to the court of the ruling sovereign to occupy the post of
Prime Minister or Regent over Egypt proper, Nubia remaining in the hands
of the *Royal Son of Kashû*. We should be better informed as to the merits
of his administration, if his panegyrist had been more sparing of formulæ
which are everywhere to be found in the inscriptions of kings or noblemen
of that period ; however, what we learn of his character as a Pharaoh, from
what he relates later on of his reforms, authorises us to believe that a considerable layer of truth is concealed under the exaggeration of the language,
and that he shewed firmness and continuity of purpose whilst in power.
Why has he not told us the name of the sovereign who called him to his
side ? If it had been Amenôthes III he would no doubt have designated
him by one or other of his cartouches, as was the custom of high Egyptian
officials in their biographies : since he is silent concerning him, is it not

---

[1] In other words, people cried the two words Health and Strength as he passed. It is not
yet the royal formula, which begins with ☥ Life, still it was much more than was allowed
for an ordinary person.

[2] Literally : " the instructed reason which the god had given to the accosting of the laws of
both countries." See above, p. 9 and note 2.

[3] See p. 6 of the present volume.

because this "king" 𓏲 ⌒ was one of those heretics of whom men wished to forget the very existence? I had imagined at first that it could not be Khuniatonu, thinking that otherwise Harmhabi would have made a tomb for himself at El-Amarna, like Aîya and perhaps Ramses.[1] On thinking it over, this reason no longer seems to me as specious as it did fifteen years ago, for, if his residence really was at Memphis, as we have reason to believe, the fact of having already a tomb at Memphis supplied him with a reason for not having another at El-Amarna. We may therefore consider it probable that the prince who conferred distinction on him and entrusted him with power was Khuniatonu, and not one of that king's short-lived successors. [2] Several museums have possessed fragments of the Memphis tomb for some time. The Leyden Museum has five, which Leemans described, without suspecting that the great lord to whom they had belonged might be the same as the Pharaoh.[3] Neither did Mariette suppose that they could be identical, but wondered whether the Harmhabi of the Cairo fragments might have been a military chief made king at Memphis for a few days through some revolution.[4] Birch was the first to guess that the Harmhabi who figures on a stela and on two door-posts from a Memphis tomb, brought to the British Museum with the Salt Collection, was no other than Pharaoh Harmhabi; [5] this Harmhabi, though not possessed of royal titles, wore, however, the uræus on his forehead, and this fact could only be explained if " he were either an " individual who had raised himself to the crown, or an independent chief, or " a king who, having been deposed, had obtained the authorisation to preserve " in his tomb the insignia of his former power."[6] He expressed his opinion in a letter which he wrote to Ed. Meyer, an extract of which is quoted by the latter in the *Zeitschrift*.[7] According to this, Harmhabi was the Pharaoh of that name " deposed but not killed by his successor, and had been " authorised to retain certain posts, as also the honours of royalty, but he died " soon after his dethronement or abdication, and was interred at Sakkara."

[1] Maspero, *La Mêlée des peuples*, p. 342, note 4.

[2] This is Breasted's opinion (*King Harmhab and his Sakkára Tomb*, in the *Zeitschrift*, 1900, vol. XXXVIII, p. 50, note 5, *Ancient Records*, vol. III, p. 13, *History of Egypt*, pp. 391, 399).

[3] Leemans, *Description raisonnée des Monuments Égyptiens*, pp. 40, 41, 1–3, and *Monuments du Musée d'Antiquités*, vol. I, Pll. XXXI–XXXIV.

[4] Mariette, *Notice des principaux Monuments*, 1864, pp. 251, 252, Nos. 74–77.

[5] Birch, *Guide to the Egyptian Galleries, Vestibule*, p. 36, Nos. 550–552; *cf.* Budge, *Guide to the Egyptian Galleries (Sculpture)*, 1909, pp. 130, 131, Nos. 461–463.

[6] Birch, *Inscription of Haremhebi*, in the *Transactions*, vol. III, p. 491.

[7] Ed. Meyer, *Die Stele des Horemheb*, in the *Zeitschrift*, 1875, pp. 148, 149.

Eduard Meyer accepted this hypothesis, but it was rejected by Wiedemann, who felt inclined to think that the personage in question was more probably some official related to the dynasty and bearing the same name as the reigning Pharaoh.[1]   Budge believes it to this day,[2] but already in 1894 I had conjectured that the terms should be reversed and that we should recognise, in the Harmhabi of the Memphis tomb, the same personage who, ascending later the throne, became Harmhabi the Pharaoh;[3] Ed. Meyer agreed with this view in 1896 in his history of Ancient Egypt.[4]   However, the proof of the identity of the two was completed in 1900 only, when Breasted discovered that a fragment of the tomb, which had found its way to Vienna, fitted the Leyden fragments.   He showed that the name-cartouche

, part of which may be read at Vienna, had been sur-charged over an older one, and also that the uræus which adorns the ruler's forehead was added afterwards, and it is difficult to see how his conclusions can be disputed.[5]   Harmhabi, having obtained supreme power, imprinted the seal of royalty on his private tomb, in the same way as, long after him, the sons of Ramses III framed their princely name in a cartouche on the colossi which stand in the first court at Medinet-Habou.

The titles of Harmhabi at Memphis are numerous and exalted.   His simpler protocol is to be found on the London stela[6]: "Hereditary Prince, Parasol-bearer to the King's right hand, Chief of the "soldiers," and "Hereditary Prince, Sole Friend, Generalis-"simo," and in the Leyden bas-reliefs "Hereditary Prince, "Sole Friend, Royal Scribe,"[7] or else "Great Favourite of the Master of both lands, real Royal Scribe whom "he loves, Major-domo."[8]   The most complete enumeration of his titles

[1] Wiedemann, *Ægyptische Geschichte*, pp. 412, 413, and *Supplement*, p. 48.

[2] Budge, *Guide to the Egyptian Galleries* (*Sculpture*), 1909, pp. 130, 131.

[3] Maspero, *Histoire Ancienne des Peuples de l'Orient*, 4th ed., p. 213, and *La Mêlée des Peuples*, 1896, p. 343, note 2.

[4] Ed. Meyer, *Geschichte des Alten Ægyptens*, pp. 271, 272.

[5] Breasted, *King Harmhab and his Sakkara Tomb*, in the *Zeitschrift*, 1900, vol. XXXVIII, pp. 47–52.

[6] The London stela has been published, transcribed and translated by Ed. Meyer, *Die Stele des Horemheb*, in the *Zeitschrift*, 1877, p. 148, and photographed by Budge, *Guide to the Egyptian Galleries* (*Sculpture*), 1909, Pl. XIX.

[7] Leemans, *Monuments du Musée d'Antiquités*, vol. I, Pl. XXXIII.

[8] *Ibid.*, vol. I, Pl. XXXIV.

is afforded to us by the fragments in Cairo and in London. Harmhabi is
styled on the Cairo slabs :

"Hereditary Prince, Chieftain, He with the King's Necklace, Sole Friend,
   " Greater than the Greatest, Mightier than the Mightiest, Supreme Chief
   " of humans,—Follower of the King in his raids in Southern and Northern
   " regions,—Prince of the greatest Royal Friends, Intimate among Intimates,
   " —Master of the Secret of the Royal Palace, He who best loves that
   " which is of his Lord, Head of the Prophets of Horus Lord of Sabi,"[1]

and

"Hereditary Prince, Chieftain, Sole Friend, King's Messenger at the head of
   " the Soldiers to the Southern and Northern regions,—King's elect,
   " leader of both countries to settle the affairs of both lands, General
   " of Generals of the soldiers of the Lord of both lands,—He who brings
   " joy to the whole land, Master of the Secret of the Royal Palace, Unique
   " in his virtues, inspector of militia,—He who guards the feet of his
   " Lord on the battle-fields on the day of killing Asiatics,"[2]

and to close each series of epithets, the current titles [hieroglyphs] "Generalis-
simo," [hieroglyphs] "real Royal Scribe who loves him," [hieroglyphs] "Major-
domo." The list of titles on the door-posts in the British Museum is
less full ; it includes, however, a few formulæ which do not figure in that
of the Cairo fragments : "Great in his Dignity, Exalted in his Office, the

---

[1] Mariette, *Monuments Divers*, Pl. 74 A ; E. and J. de Rougé, *Inscriptions hiéroglyphiques*,
Pl. CVII ; the text has been translated by Breasted, *Ancient Records of Egypt*, vol. III, pp. 11, 12.

[2] Mariette, *Monuments Divers*, Pl. 74 B ; E. and J. de Rougé, *Inscriptions hiéroglyphiques*,
Pl. CVIII ; the text has been translated by Breasted, *Ancient Records of Egypt*, vol. III, p. 12.

" King's Two eyes in the Two countries, He who satisfies the King in all
" monuments, and who directs the works at the Granite Mountain."[1]   Petrie
has compared the titles assumed by Harmhabi in his tomb and the functions
which he declares himself to have exercised in the inscription of the Turin
statue, and he proves that the two monuments agree in every point of their
testimony.[2]

The identity being established, it becomes easy to extract from the remains of
the tomb some items of information regarding various episodes of Harmhabi's
administration prior to his accession to the throne.   The most important are
those which concern his relations with the peoples of Syria.   Leemans gives
us faithful reproductions of them, as I have already mentioned.[3]   Breasted
gave them their full value when he connected the Vienna fragment
with them.[4]   The subject is the set of golden ornaments which the king
granted to his minister to reward him for his services in Egypt and in
foreign lands.   In one of the scenes the upper register is almost completely
destroyed, but we can guess by the traces that remain that a troop of horses,
probably a tribute from some Asiatic prince, is being led before the king.
In the lower register which alone remains, Harmhabi, his hands raised in joy,
receives the gold necklets whilst, behind him, in two long rows, Asiatic
prisoners or hostages come forward, each between two Egyptians.[5]   In the
other scene Harmhabi stands before the royal couple whose heads and busts
have disappeared.   The characteristics of the figures are the same as at
El-Amarna.   Moreover, he is wearing the necklets, and we can read in front
of his figure the last words of four lines running thus :

---

[1] The inscriptions on these door-posts have been published by Sharpe, *Egyptian Inscriptions*,
vol. II, p. 92, and entirely translated by Breasted, *Ancient Records of Egypt*, vol. III, pp. 8–10.

[2] Flinders Petrie, *A History of Egypt*, vol. III, 3rd edition, 1904, p. 244.

[3] Leemans, *Monuments du Musée d'Antiquités*, vol. I, Pll. XXXI–XXXIV.   See p. 12, note 3.

[4] Breasted, *King Harmhab and his Sakkara Tomb*, in the *Zeitschrift*, 1900, vol. XXVII,
p. 47.

[5] Leemans, *Monuments du Musée d'Antiquités*, vol. I, Pl. XXXI, and Breasted–Ranke,
Geschichte Ægyptens, Figs. 116, 117.

[6] *Cf.* above, p. 9, l. 7, of the inscription, .

" (Words spoken to the King) unto him, the Hereditary Prince, Sole Friend,
     " Scribe Harmhabi, He of the true voice. He said, replying (to his
     " Majesty : ' Royalty is thine) for ever and for ever, for Amen has given
     " it unto thee by a decree. They push (every) foreign country (and
     " they all submit to thee) in their hearts as if they were but one. Thy
     " name is a fire (against them) . . . .' " [1]

On the right of this scene is the beginning of another, in which we perceive
Harmhabi, adorned with his necklets, walking towards a group of his
servants, Asiatics or Egyptians, whose joy is expressed by animated
gestures ; behind the first group three rows of native or foreign slaves are
coming to meet him.[2] A third scene, which was depicted above the latter,
has been preserved for us by the precious fragment in Vienna. The figure of
Harmhabi which was on the left hand of the register is now lost, but a
group of officials, bowing before him, is well preserved ; they appear to
be listening with respect to the words which fall from the lips of the Chief.
It must have been fairly long, but only the lower part of seven lines remains,
just enough for us to understand the meaning of the whole :

" Asiatic Barbarians and others have been put in their places ; . . . . . (their
     " pastures) have been destroyed, their city has been sacked, and fire
     " has been set (to their harvests . . . . . so that they came to implore)

---

[1] Leemans, *Monuments du Musée d'Antiquités*, vol. I, Pl. XXXIII.

[2] Leemans, *Monuments du Musée d'Antiquités*, vol. I, Pl. XXIV. Breasted–Ranke, *Geschichte
Ægyptens*, Fig. 147 ; Breasted, *King Harmhab and his Sakkara Tomb*, in the *Zeitschrift*, 1900,
vol. XXXVII, p. 47.

" the Mighty One[1] to send his powerful sword towards (them) . . . .

" . . . Their lands are starving, they live like the goats of the mountains,

" (their) children . . . . (They have therefore sent), saying : 'Some

" Asiatic Barbarians, no longer knowing how to live, have come (to beg

" for a place where they might settle down) from Pharaoh, l. h. s.,

" according to the custom of your fathers' fathers, since Creation, under

" . . . . . .' And Pharaoh, l. h. s., hands them over to you, in order

" that you should protect their frontiers."

The Asiatics stood on the right hand, on a block now lost, but we still have the end of the first line of their legend : saying that "they are worshipping " the Good God, the Strong One, Zaskhuprurîya-Satpanrîya."[2]

Breasted has shown that the cartouche was a surcharge over an anterior cartouche which can hardly have been other than that of Khuniatonu, for the outline of the King and Queen as figured on the Sakkâra tomb is identical with that of the sovereigns of El-Amarna.[3] The circumstances which turned those unhappy Asiatics from their country to the land of Egypt were no doubt those alluded to by Setuî I in the inscription at Karnak, where his campaign of the year I is depicted[4] : the disturbance caused in Syria by the conquests of the Khati and the momentary decline of the power of Egypt were the origin of the trouble. In Ethiopia, at the other extremity of the Empire, Harmhabi's activity proved no less efficacious, and a fragment, which found its way to the Bologna Museum with the collection of the painter Palaggi, pictures him engaged in presenting a troop of negroes to the king, whilst a tribute from Palestine is mentioned in the inscription.[5] It is probably this episode which formed the subject of the text gathered by

---

[1] Meaning the reigning Pharaoh.

[2] This picture has twice been published by Breasted, *King Harmhab and his Sakkara Tomb*, in the *Zeitschrift*, 1900, vol. XXXVII, p. 47, and *Geschichte Ægyptens*, Fig. 147 ; the text has been transcribed and translated by A. Wiedemann, *Texts of the Second Part of the XVIIIth Dynasty*, in the *Proceedings of the Society of Biblical Archæology*, 1889, vol. XI, p. 423, and by Bergmann, *Ansiedlungen Semitischer Nomaden in Ægypten*, in the *Zeitschrift*, 1889, vol. XXVII, p. 126.

[3] Breasted, *King Harmhab and his Sakkara Tomb*, in the *Zeitschrift*, 1900, vol. XXXVII, p. 49. There is, however, a remote chance that the king may be Touatânkhamanou, whose name we know Harmhabi to have replaced with his own in several instances.

[4] Lepsius, *Denkmäler*, III, 126a.

[5] Breasted recognised the origin of this fragment (*Ancient Records of Egypt*, vol. III, p. 12); the scene and text have hitherto not been published.

Wiedemann on the Alexandria fragment, and which runs above a figure of Harmhabi standing, the uræus on his forehead. It seems from the first line to refer to an expedition up the Nile :

"He was sent as a Royal messenger to the place where the discus Atonu
"shineth ; going, he triumphed . . . . and no land holds
"before him, but he seized them in the space of a moment, so that his
"name is repeated in the lands of the (Southerners). He returned to
"the North, and behold His Majesty appeared on the dais which is used
"for the presentation of the tributes, and the tributes of the South and of
"the North passed before him, and, behold, Prince Harmhabi stood at
"the side (of the dais) worshipping His (Majesty)." [1]

Several stray blocks in the Bologna and Cairo Museums have no special historical interest ; they show us Harmhabi, the uræus on his forehead, kneeling before the gods of the dead,[2] or ploughing the fields of Ialou.[3] Those which I have now described and interpreted at length prove to us that Harmhabi really filled the posts which he ascribes to himself in the inscription on the Turin group : he had already had a long and honourable career when he was called upon to assume the crown.

[1] The text has been published and translated by Wiedemann, *Texts of the Second Part of the XVIIIth Dynasty*, in the *Proceedings of the Society of Biblical Archæology*, 1889, vol. XI, p. 424, and then translated again by Breasted, *Ancient Records of Egypt*, vol. III, p. 8.

[2] Mariette, *Monuments Divers*, Pl. 75 ; E. and J. de Rougé, *Inscriptions hiéroglyphiques*, Pll. CIV–VI.

[3] Breasted, *Ancient Records of Egypt*, p. 12, and *Geschichte Ægyptens*, Fig. 149, where a portion of the scene is reproduced in zincogravure.

§ III.—THE ACCESSION AND CORONATION OF HARMHABI.

We do not know how it was that the power passed into the hands of Harmhabi when the throne became vacant after the death of Aîya. The inscription on the Turin group, the only document which relates the accession, gives a purely conventional account of events:

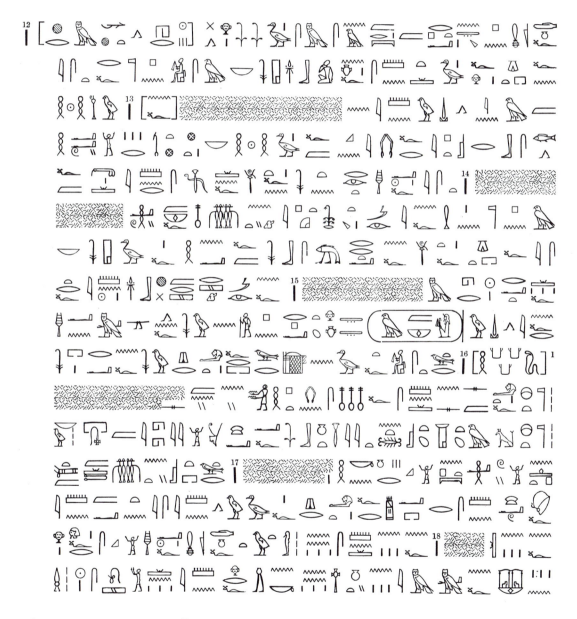

[1] Restitution by Sethe, *Der angebliche Bericht über Harmhabs Verheiratung in seiner Thronbesteigungsinschrift*, in the *Zeitschrift*, 1907, vol. XCIV, pp. 35, 36.

" (Now when the days) had passed, the eldest son of Horus being Supreme
" Chief and Hereditary Prince in this whole land, behold the August
" God, Horus, Master of Hasoute, his heart wished that his son should
" be established on his Eternal Throne and he commanded . . . .
" of . . . . . of Amon. Horus therefore proceeded joyfully to Thebes,
" the city of the Master of Eternity, holding his son in his embrace;
" and to Karnak, in order that he should present himself before
" Amon and that the latter should transmit unto him his kingly
" office, and that he should spend his existence (in that quality).
" Behold, (Amon, King of the Gods came) rejoicing[2] to his fair feast
" at Luxor, he saw the Majesty of the God Horus, Master of Hasoute,
" and his son with him who presented himself (to him, Amon),
" in order that Amon should give him his office and his throne;
" and behold Amonrîya was filled with joy when he saw him (as he
" presented himself) on the day of thank-offerings. He passed there-
" fore before this Lord, Hereditary Prince, Chief of both Lands,

---

[1] Birch, *Inscription of Haremhebi on a Statue at Turin*, in the *Transactions of the Society of Biblical Archæology*, p. 486; and Brugsch, *Thesaurus Inscriptionum Ægyptiacarum*, vol. V, pp. 1076–1077.

[2] This restitution is indicated by the passage in lines 21, 22, where it is said that "having ended the feast at Luxor, Amon went in peace to Thebes-Karnak ⸢⸣." In order that Amon could return to Luxor it is necessary that he should have come therefrom, and the only place in the inscription where this coming can have been mentioned is precisely the beginning of line 15, where three or four words are missing.

" Harmhabi, he betook himself to the palace, he placed himself before
" the sanctuary of his august daughter, the Great (Magician). She
." saluted (the Prince) bowing her back and her hands, she embraced his
" beauties, she clung to his forehead, and the Gods, Masters of the *Fiery
" Hall*, shouted with joy because of his coronation. Nekhabît, Wazît,
" Neith, Isis, Nephthys, Horus, Set, the complete *Ennead* of Gods
" which preside over the great Place, (raised) acclamations Heaven high,
" exulting in Amon's satisfaction : ' Now behold, Amon has come, with
" his son before him, to the Palace, to place his diadem on his head and
" to lengthen the duration of his whole life. We assembled and we
" establish (him in) the (kingship), we (give) him the ornaments of the
" Sun and we praise Amon on his account. Thou hast brought unto
" us Him who protects us. Grant unto him the feasts, periods of the
" Sun and the years of Horus as King, for he it is who will delight
" thy heart at Karnak and also at Heliopolis and Memphis, he it is who
" makes those cities august. May the great name of this Good God
" and his protocol be established like that of the Sun, *Horus Mighty
" Bull, rich in good projects, the crowned by the two Divine Queens, Very
" Miraculous in Karnak, the Victorious Horus who finds his delight in
" Justice, who makes both Lands live, King of both Egypts, Záskhu-
" prurîya, Son of the Sun, Harmhabi-Maîamánou, the Vivified.'* Then
" the Majesty of this August God, Amonrâsonthêr having come forth to
" the Audience Hall of the Palace, with his son before him, he
" embraced his beauties, crowned as he was with the royal helmet, to
" transmit unto him the circuit of the Solar Disc, the Barbarians under
" his feet, Heaven feasting, the Earth rejoicing, the Ennead of the Gods
" of Egypt their hearts content. Now behold, the whole people rejoiced
" and their cries resounded in the Heavens, great and small they
" rejoiced and the whole earth exulted."

Brugsch was, as far as I know, the first to believe that the fifteenth and
sixteenth lines of the inscription contained an allusion to Harmhabi's
marriage with one of Amon's daughters, that is, with a Princess of the Royal
family ; himself a usurper, he would have legalized his usurpation by
marrying the heiress of the Ahmessides.[1] Egyptologists for the most part
adopted his opinion, and even those who like myself supposed that the
union mentioned in this passage was that of Amon with Nazmimaut never

---

[1] Brugsch, *Geschichte Ægyptens*, p. 439.

doubted but that a real person was alluded to.[1] To Sethe belongs the merit of demonstrating that this was not an allusion to a marriage, and that the daughter of Amon to whom the God presented Harmhabi was a goddess, [hieroglyphs], *Werît-haqau*, Lady of Charms and Enchantments, the uræus which shines on the forehead of Pharaoh.[2] The scribe who wrote our inscription relates in the mythological manner the principal scene of the coronation, in which the new sovereign receives on his head the diadems or the helmet ornamented with the uræus. We must therefore take away from our histories every hypothesis which had been introduced in consequence of the faulty interpretation momentarily given to this passage of the inscription, and content ourselves with seeing in it an act of the solemn ceremony of enthronement. Harmhabi, who had probably started from Memphis, where the seat of his government was established,[3] arrived at Luxor whilst Amon was there, in order to celebrate the great annual patronal feast of that city, [hieroglyphs]. Perhaps we have here some means of knowing about what time in the year the official consecration of the new sovereign's supreme power took place. Amon's feast at Luxor, which lasted for twenty-four days, began, according to the fragment of the Elephantine calendar, on the fifteenth of the second month of Akhaît, under Thoutmôsis III, [hieroglyphs], and another feast of Amon of which the name is mutilated, was celebrated a few days later, on the ninth of the third month of Akhaît, [hieroglyphs], probably that of Amon of Karnak.[4] About two and a half centuries later, under Ramses III, at Medinet Habou, we see that the nineteenth of the second month of Akhaît was the first day of the feast of Amon at Thebes, [hieroglyphs], and this lasted twenty-four whole days until the twelfth of the third month of Akhaît, after which came, on the nineteenth of that same third month, another feast, that which followed the feast of Thebes, [hieroglyphs] [hieroglyphs].[5] Without searching here for the exact moment in which

[1] Maspero, *Struggle of the Nations*, p. 342, notes 2, 3.

[2] K. Sethe, *Der angebliche Bericht über Harmhabs Verheiratung in seiner Thronbesteigungsinschrift*," in the *Zeitschrift*, 1907, vol. XLIV, pp. 35, 36.

[3] See above, p. 12 *sqq.*

[4] Brugsch, *Thesaurus Inscriptionum Ægyptiacarum*, p. 363, *c*, Pll. 3, 4.

[5] Brugsch, *Thesaurus Inscriptionum Ægyptiacarum*, p. 364.

the reign of Harmhabi fell between those two dates, we may suppose that in his time the first day of the first of those feasts, that which coincided with his arrival at Thebes and his presentation to Amon, was about half-way between the fifteenth of the second month of Akhaît and the nineteenth of the third month, that is to say, supposing there had been no alteration made to the calendar in the interval, about the first of the third month of Akhaît.

Curiously enough it has occurred to no one until now to illustrate our inscription by means of the scenes which adorn the two walls between which lies the gigantic column of the Luxor temple. They represent a feast of Amon : Amon is coming forth from his sanctuary on his way to the sanctuary of the neighbouring town, and, the ceremonies having been performed, he is seen returning to the place whence he started. Daressy, who first became acquainted with these scenes and who published them,[1] had already noticed that on their way out the ships had all their sails unfurled and were therefore sailing up stream, whilst on the return journey they were drifting down the river. He had concluded therefrom that the departure took place from Karnak and that Amon went up to visit Luxor.[2] All Egyptologists have adopted this opinion, and I see no reason to contest it, but they do not all agree as to the identity of the sovereign for whom those bas-reliefs were executed. Daressy thought they were done for Harmhabi, Amenôthes III having erected the walls but having had no time to decorate them, so that the glory of doing so was left to Harmhabi.[3] Borchardt, Budge, and Breasted[4] consider that the whole ornamentation dates from the reign of Touatânkha-manou, Harmhabi having appropriated it by substituting his cartouches for those of his predecessor. My examination of the monuments does not allow me to adopt completely the latter hypothesis ; it led me to believe that those cartouches of Harmhabi which are still legible were not always engraved over cartouches of another king, but that some at least were traced on a virgin surface. Even should I be mistaken on this point, and had the whole thing been usurped by Harmhabi, this monument would still be of the greatest value in relation to the history of his accession. The annual feast of Amon was

---

[1] G. Daressy, *La procession d'Ammon dans le temple de Louxor*, in the *Mémoires publiés par les membres de la Mission Archéologique française au Caire*, vol. VIII, pp. 380–391, Pll. I–XVI.

[2] G. Daressy, *La procession d'Ammon*, p. 390.

[3] G. Daressy, *La procession d'Ammon*, pp. 390, 391.

[4] Borchardt, *Zur Geschichte des Luxortempels*, in the *Zeitschrift*, 1896, vol. XXXIV, pp. 131, 134–136 ; Budge, *A History of Egypt*, vol. IV, p. 143 ; Breasted, *A History of Egypt*, p. 393.

celebrated according to immutable rites, and the person of the sovereign was but a variable accessory, but the fact that the arrival in Thebes of the prince who restored Amon's cult should have coincided with this feast was too remarkable to be left unnoticed. In the coronation inscription this fact affords the subject of a paragraph ; the Luxor walls, if they were not decorated with the special intention of commemorating it, were certainly used advisedly for that purpose by the priests. Even supposing that Harmhabi merely utilised an older composition, he had only to inscribe his name on it to effect that, what had been destined for another, should become an exact representation of what had taken place for himself. Moreover, some expressions here and there apply directly to his case. For instance, in the place where, in Karnak, burning incense is offered to the royal ship ⟨hieroglyphs⟩, we read the following legend above the head of the king :

⟨hieroglyphic text⟩ [1]

"The good God, son of Amon, whom this god set as a king on his throne,
      "King of Upper and Lower Egypt, Ruler of both lands, Zaskhuprurîya
      "Satpanrîya, whom Amon loved more than any king."

There is perhaps no special purpose in the first words, but the last have an unusual look, and acquire a special value when we remember that Harmhabi worked vigorously for the restoration of the cult of Amon. I therefore think we are justified in using these scenes to throw light upon the coronation inscription.

They are a good deal damaged on either side of the double row of columns. The first one at the northern extremity of the west wall shows us the interior of the Karnak sanctuary, the four divine ships still lying on their supports, that of Amon, the *Was-hai* ⟨hieroglyphs⟩, above, those of the king, of Maut and of Khonsu in the inferior register. The king sacrifices to the gods, who reward him by granting him all that is necessary to a mighty king—Life, Truth, Strength, the Sovereignty of both worlds, of durable monuments, Perfect Joy.[2] In the second picture, the façade of the temple appears as it was then,

---

[1] G. Daressy, *La procession d'Ammon*, p. 382. The same expression is found, applied to Amenôthes I by one of Harmhabi's contemporaries, ⟨hieroglyphs⟩ (Champollion, *Monuments de l'Égypte et de la Nubie*, p. 549) "the excellent child of Amon whom he loved more than any king."

[2] G. Daressy, *La procession d'Ammon*, pp. 380, 381, Pl. I.

Amenôthes III's façade, now hidden by the eastern wall of the Hypostyle Hall. The ships sail out in the artificial wind of fans ; Amon's ship, Harmhabi walking behind it, is in the upper register : in the lower we see those of the king, of Maut and of Khonsu.[1] Having reached the bank of the Nile, probably about the spot where is now the rest-house of the Service des Antiquités, the sacred barques are placed on boats patiently towed by a crowd of labourers running along the shore, whilst a priest sings the praises of Amon :

" Thy rising is fair, Amonrîya, for whilst thou art in the Was-haî barque, the
   " whole people acclaim thee, the whole earth is rejoicing, and thy son
   " has opened the wharf that thou mayst go to Luxor," etc.

A detachment of Egyptian soldiers marches behind the priest, then come "His Majesty's great horses" harnessed to the two empty chariots of the king and queen, then the towing-men, in strained attitudes, then four negro mountebanks and some dancing Timihou with their two head-feathers. This is Amon's suite ; that of Maut begins with four priestesses escorted by four men, and closes with a company of officers bearing banners, and some soldiers leaping along in their haste. All these people repeat unto satiety that they are going to the feast of Luxor, , the august city which was the seat of the God of Creation, .[2] At Luxor, the sacred barques are laid on the ground, taken up, carried to the temple, and placed on their pedestals in the sanctuary in order to receive the homage of Harmhabi.[3] The return to Karnak is depicted along the east wall : the king, who alone has the privilege of seeing the gods face to face, is completing the acts of worship, whilst the officers of the crown are waiting for him outside the door. As soon as he has done his part, the priests raise the barques again on their shoulders and bring them down to the river : they place them in their boats, and the towing begins anew in the opposite direction, with the same rites :

---

[1] G. Daressy, *La procession d'Ammon*, pp. 381, 382, Pll. II and III.
[2] G. Daressy, *La procession d'Ammon*, pp. 381–384, Pll. III–VI.
[3] G. Daressy, *La procession d'Ammon*, pp. 384, 385, Pll. VI–VIII.

"The fields are rejoicing, the earth is feasting, the city of Thebes is full of
"joy, because Zaskhprurîya Satpanrîya is bringing back his father
"Amon to rest in Karnak."

The king convoys Amon, the queen convoys Maut, and on this occasion we
learn her full protocol from the text:

"Great Hereditary Princess, Lady of Grace, Sweetness of Love unto the
"South and unto the North, Priestess who holds the god's sistrum in
"every place, Most Loving, Always Shining unto whom Maut gave her
"form to increase Love, Great Queen, ... Lady
"of both lands, Nazmimaut, brings (her mother Maut) Lady of Heaven,
"to this good feast of Karnak."[1]

Re-entering the temple they receive the highest honours and the feast ends
as it began by Royal offerings.[2]

§ IV.—THE KNOWN DATES OF THE REIGN OF HARMHABI.

Not many dates of Harmhabi's reign are known to us; six only have been
ascertained to this day: (1) the date of the first year of his reign on the
temple of Theban-Phtah in Karnak[3]:

---

[1] G. Daressy, *La procession d'Ammon*, pp. 385–388, Pll. IX–XIV.

[2] G. Daressy, *La procession d'Ammon*, pp. 388–390, Pll. XIV–XVI.

[3] Mariette, *Karnak*, Pl. 47 *d* and p. 74 in the text; H. Brugsch, *Recueil de Monuments*, vol. I,
Pl. XXXVII, and *Thesaurus Inscriptionum Ægyptiacarum*, pp. 1223, 1224.

" In the year 1, the fourth month of Akhaît, the twenty-second day, of King
" Zaskhuprurîya Satpanrîya, Son· of the Sun, Harmhabi Maîamânu,
" vivified,—Day. of the feast of Phtah-rîsanbuf, Ruler of Ankhtaui in
" Thebes at her feast . . . ."

The first name of the king had been engraved originally on a coat of stucco,
which hid the junction of four blocks ; the stucco having fallen away, the
name was engraved afresh after a time, and this led M. Legrain to conclude
that it was surcharged over the name of Touatânkhamanou.[1] I think that this
was a Ptolemaïc restoration, and that the original really dates from Harmhabi's
reign, even from the very beginning of it.   For if, as I have suggested above,[2]
the accession of the sovereign and the feasts of Amon with which it coincided
were celebrated about the first day of the third month of Akhaît, the feast
of Phtah of Thebes, falling on the twenty-second day of the fourth month
in the same season, took place less than two months after Harmhabi ascended
the throne.   The choice and appointment of the members of the priesthood, the
enumeration of whom formed the main part of the inscription, must have
taken place during the interval.

(2) The date of the third year, in the tomb of *Amon's Divine Father*,
Nafhatpé at El-Assassif.   Nothing in the remains of Nafhatpé's tomb shows
us what he had done to deserve the award of the golden necklets.   He was
attached to the worship of Amon, and it may have been on account of the
services he rendered when the cult was restored ; in any case, the ceremony
of his investiture is briefly depicted on one of the walls.[3]   It was at the close
of an audience held in the *Golden Hall* ▭ at the *Door of Life and Power*
▭▭ that the king appeared, according to the rites, on the balcony·
of the kiosk generally used on similar occasions.   He wore the helmet ▭
and carried in his left hand the whip ▭ and crook ▭, and he raised his

[1] Legrain, *Le temple de Ptah-ris-anbou-f dans Thebes*, in the *Annales du Service des Antiquités*,
vol. III, p. 41.

[2] See above, p. 22 *sqq*.

[3] It has been reproduced in colours and published by G. Bénédite, *Le tombeau de
Neferhotpou*, in the *Mémoires de la Mission française au Caire*, vol. V, Pl. VI, and the
inscriptions translated, pp. 496–498, and reproduced in hieroglyphics, p. 534, note 2;
cf. Brugsch, *Recueil de Monuments*, Pl. XXXVII, and Dümichen, *Historische Inschriften*, vol. II,
Pl. XL *e*.   The inscription has also been translated by Pierret, *L'investiture du Collier*, in the
Mélanges d'Archéologie Égyptienne et Assyrienne, vol. II, pp. 196, 197, and by Amélineau, *Un
tombeau Égyptien*, in the *Revue de l'Histoire des Religions*, 1891, vol. XXIII, pp. 141, 142, and
lastly by Breasted, *Ancient Records of Egypt*, vol. III, pp. 33, 34.

right hand as he stood in the attitude of a man addressing a crowd : two persons stood behind him, carrying the long-handled flabellum 𓉺𓏶𓏶 two "grooms of the chamber, the King's cup-bearers, who follow "the King wherever he goes." A small table upon which might be seen the necklets and armlets stood a little in front of the platform : the Head of the White House Maîya 𓉺𓏶, escorted by his two acolytes the 𓉺𓏶 "poliarchs of the South and the North," directly receives the orders of the Sovereign, whilst, behind him, two ushers place the gold necklets and belt round the neck and waist of Nafhatpé. The scene is described in eighteen lines of the inscription :

[hieroglyphic inscription of eighteen lines, numbered 1–18]

" In the year 3, under the Majesty of the King of Both Egypts, Zaskhprurîya
" Satpanrîya, behold, His Majesty rose like unto the Sun in his *Door*
" *of Life and Power*, after making the offering of loaves unto his father
" Amon and coming forth from the *Golden Hall;* acclamations and
" genuflections went round the whole earth, the noise of rejoicing
" reached unto Heaven when Nafhatpé, the Divine Father of Amon, was
" called to receive the favours of the King, millions of all things, silver,
" gold, dresses, oils, loaves, beers, meats, cakes, 'according to the order
" of my father Amon, who has manifested my favours in the presence
" of all.'[1]   Thus speaks the man with the scroll, who is pleasing unto
" Amon, saying : 'He is rich who knoweth the gifts of His God, the

---

[1] Here Nafhatpé suddenly passes from direct to indirect speech.

"King of Gods, a God Who knoweth whoever knoweth Him, Who
"favours whoever worketh for Him, Who protects whoever serveth Him,
"for He is Rîya, the Discus is His body, and He exists unto Eternity.'"

Having thus spoken, Nafhatpé retires, wearing his gold necklets, and he is
greeted first by his brother Amanamauné, then by Prinnâfa, both being his
colleagues in the priesthood of Amon:

[hieroglyphic text]

"'The Divine Father of Amon, Amanamauné his brother, the Divine Father
"of Amon, Nafhatpé, rewarded in silver and in gold by the King himself,
"he cometh in peace with the royal favours' (said) the Divine Father of
"Amon, Prinnâfa."

(3) The dates of the seventh and the twenty-first years, on Ostracon
No. 5624 in the British Museum:[1]

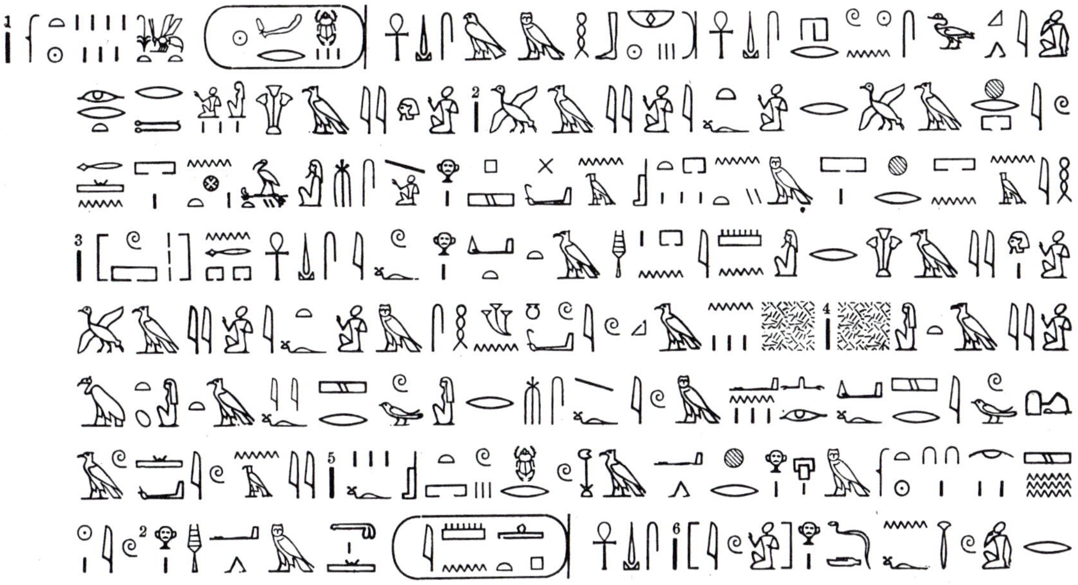

[hieroglyphic text]

¹ It was published by Birch, *Inscriptions in the Hieratic and Demotic Characters*, Pl. XIV,
and translated by Brugsch, *Geschichte Ægyptens*, pp. 447, 448, after being transcribed in
hieroglyphics by the same in 1876, in the *Zeitschrift, die Gruppe man*, pp. 122–124, and
partly analysed by Goodwin, *On the word* [glyphs], in the *Zeitschrift*, 1872, pp. 30, 31.

² The text offers [glyphs], and the sense requires that we should read [glyphs]: it is possible,
however, that the pronoun for the 1st person had already disappeared at that epoch and that
the spelling [glyphs] answered to the new pronunciation, but even if that is the case, it would be
against the rules of writing in force at that time. There are other examples in texts from
the same period, such as the Misé inscription, North Wall, lines 10, 12.

Here ends on the front side the legible portion of the document. The seven lines to be found on the back are not sufficiently clear on the facsimile to enable me to venture on a transcription of them. We may gather from them that a third person interferes, who seems to have endeavoured to identify the site of the restored lands or perhaps to appropriate them. His action takes place at two different days in the same month of the twenty-first year and [1] Here is a translation of the legible parts of this text:

"In the year 7 of King Zaskhuprurîya, l. h. s., Harmhabu, l. h. s. On the
"day when men laid my father Hâîya in the cemetery, the governor of
"the town, Thoutmôsis, divided the sites which are in the necropolis
"of the *daïrah* of Pharaoh, l. h. s., and he gave Amon's concession to
"Haîya my father as his property, for my mother Qan . . . . . was his
"daughter born unto him, and he had no male child and his sites
"remained abandoned. Now, subsequently, in the year 21, on the
"first day of the second month of Shomu, I appeared before Amenô-
"thes, l. h. s., and I said unto him : 'Assign unto each the concessions
"of his father !' and he gave me the concessions of Haîya my father by
"an authentic deed, and forthwith I began to work upon the land
"thereof."

There is nothing historical about this document, but it is an interesting instance of the customs of the time. A certain Haîya died in the year 7 of Harmhabi's reign, and, since he possessed no family tomb, was buried in a concession belonging to one Thoutmôsis, his wife's father ; but, the latter having no male child, the remainder of his concession was lost. Fourteen years having passed, the son of Haîya, Thoutmôsis's grandson, goes to Amenôthes, l. h. s., to claim the lost concession : Amenôthes grants it and he sets to work upon it. The sequel is of little importance ; the question is, who was this Amenôthes, and does the date of the year 21 refer to him

---

[1] Birch, *Egyptian Inscriptions*, Pl. XIV, *Reverse of No.* 5624, lines 2 and 4 ; in the second case the number is written half in red ink and half in black.

or to Harmhabi? Birch, who was the first to publish the ostracon, had no hesitation in identifying Amenôthes with the Pharaoh Amenôthes III, and in crediting his reign with the date 21: according to him, Haîya's son was looking back upon the past years, and claiming a site of which the ownership or enjoyment had been granted to his family fifty years previously, in the year 21 of Amenôthes III.[1] Birch's opinion was immediately adopted by Goodwin,[2] but rejected by Brugsch, who assigned the date to Harmhabi's reign, and who, in spite of the cartouche which frames the name of Amenôthes, refused to admit that the bearer of it was one of the Pharaohs.[3] Since then it has been almost unanimously agreed to consider the date as belonging to Harmhabi without troubling further as to the identity of Amenôthes, and prudently putting aside all the other questions suggested by his name.[4] If we examine the circumstances in which this name appears, we find firstly that, without having a complete protocol, he still possesses the cartouche followed by the formula 𓋹𓍑𓋴, Life, Health, Strength; and secondly that litigations occurring in Pharaoh's necropolis are submitted to him, that he decides concerning them, and that his decisions become law. Only one personality answers to these two conditions, that of Amenôthes I, the second of the great sovereigns of the XVIIIth Dynasty. He had then been dead for a long time, but he had become a god, and, together with his wife Ahmasi-Naftera, received regular worship. He had become the patron, first of the portion of the Theban necropolis where his funeral monument stood, then of the entire necropolis. We have brought to the Cairo Museum a papyrus which contains the ritual of his cult; he came forth in procession on his solemn feast-day, and, like the other gods his peers, rendered oracles and delivered judgment in all the affairs which concerned the Theban cemeteries. Now the question here was the recovering possession of the *wakf* of a place of burial and, if he really was the *nazir* of all those *wakfs*, as it seems to me from various texts that he was, it is conceivable that the son of Haîya should have applied to him to obtain his rights. It was probably in a form similar to that used by Amon of Karnak when some cause was pleaded before him[5]; he restored to the claimant the property which he had lost. The presence of the name of Amenôthes on Ostracon No. 5624 is thus naturally explained

[1] Birch, *Inscriptions in the Hieratic and Demotic Character*, pp. 6, 7.

[2] Goodwin, *On the word*, in the *Zeitschrift*, 1872, pp. 30, 31.

[3] Brugsch, *Geschichte Ægyptens*, pp. 447, 448.

[4] For instance, Wiedemann, *Ægyptische Geschichte*, p. 411; Flinders Petrie, *A History of Egypt*, vol. II, p. 251.

[5] *Cf.* the account published by E. Naville, *Inscription de Pinodjem III*, 1885.

and the date of the year 21 remains Harmhabi's. We shall presently examine under what conditions it was so.

(4) The date of the year 8 in the tomb of Thoutmôsis IV at Bibân-el-Muluk. It is inscribed at the beginning of a graffito traced in fine hieratics, in black ink, on the right-hand wall of the second chamber in the hypogeum of that prince.[1] Here is a transcription of it in hieroglyphic characters :

and this first inscription is completed by another, giving the name of the scribe :

" In the year 8, on the first day of the third month of Akhaît, under the
    " Majesty of the King of both Egypts, Zaskhupruriya, Son of the Sun,
    " Harmhabi Maîamânu, His Majesty, l. h. s., ordered that the flabellum-
    " bearer on the King's right hand, Royal Scribe, Over Steward of the
    " Double White House, Over Steward of the Works of the Eternal Place,
    " Leader of the Feast of Amon in Karnak, Maîya, son of the Master
    " Auî, born of the lady Werît, should be requested to renew the
    " funereal equipage of King Mankhupruriya, of the True Voice, in the
    " august residence situated east of Thebes "

— " His adjutant, the Steward of the City of the South, Thoutmôsis, son of
    " Hatiyaia, whose mother is Yuha, of the city."

The two graffiti concern the inspection made in the Bab-el-Muluk by order of the Pharaoh Harmhabi. It is difficult to say to what degree the tomb of Thoutmôsis IV had suffered. The state in which it was found by Davis

---

[1] Th. Davis, *The Tomb of Thoutmôsis IV*, pp. xxxiii, xxxiv, Fig. 7, with a transcription in hieroglyphics and a translation by Newberry.

when the latter entered it in 1904 must evidently have been the doing of robbers of the Ramesside period, and I do not think that Maîya and Thoutmôsis his adjutant met with anything like such disorder. If it had been so, they would have mentioned it; as they merely say that they were sent by the sovereign to renew the funereal paraphernalia of his predecessor, it is probable that they did what had to be done and left the hypogeum in fairly good condition.

(5) The date of the year 59, in the inscription on the tomb of Masé at Sakkâra.[1] Several times in this inscription some allusion is made to facts dating from the reign of Harmhabi 𓄿𓏤𓅯𓏤𓏏𓈖𓈖𓏏𓆑𓅐𓏏𓆯𓏏𓈖𓁶 [2] but only one bears a fixed date, a decree rendered by the Assembly of Notables:

𓏤𓈖𓈖𓏤𓏤𓏤𓏤𓏤 [3] 𓇳𓇋𓁐𓀁 𓇳𓆣𓅱 𓇳𓅆 𓇋𓏏𓈖𓅐𓂓

" in the year 59[3] under the Majesty of the King of both Egypts, Zaskhupru-
" rîya, Son of the Sun, Harmhabi Maiamânu."[4]

The two dates of the year 21 and the year 59 have not been adopted without some discussion. Petrie, who thinks that there is no reason to doubt the exactness of the numbers of years attributed by Manetho and his abbreviators to each reign of the XVIIIth Dynasty, is made uneasy by these dates. Julius Africanus ascribes five years to Armais, or more strictly, according to Josephus, four years and one month; if those figures are correct, as he believes them to be, what can the year 8, the year 21, and, let us add, the year 59 possibly be? He sees but one solution to the problem thus stated, and that is that Harmhabi dated his monuments from his accession to the throne at first, and later, when he had completely abolished the worship of Atonu, from the time when the cult of Amon was re-established under Touatânkhamanou. The Ostracon No. 5624, which is dated from the year 21 and in which the year 7 is mentioned, would,

---

[1] Discovered and published by Loret, *La Grande Inscription de Mes à Saqqarah*, in the *Zeitschrift*, 1901, vol. XXXIX, pp. 1–10, translated and commented upon by Moret, *Un Procès de Famille sous la XIXᵉ Dynastie*, in the *Zeitschrift*, 1901, vol. XXXIX, pp. 11–39, and by Gardiner, *the Inscription of Mes, a Contribution to Egyptian Judicial Procedure*, in 4to, Leipzig, 1905.

[2] Inscription on the North panel, lines 3, 11.

[3] Perhaps 58, the expression being divided into two parts, the first part being engraved at the end of a line, and the four last units being carried over to the beginning of the following line; however, Loret's reading seems almost certain, *La Grande Inscription de Mes à Saqqarah*, p. 4.

[4] Inscriptions on the South panel, line 8.

6

according to this theory, belong in reality to the year 5 of his reign proper,
and would mention the year 3 of the reign of Aîya, considered as the year 7
of Harmhabi.[1]   On the other hand, Loret, in his publication of the inscription
of the year 59, expresses some astonishment at such a high figure in relation
to the reign of a sovereign " of whom we did not even dare to affirm that he
" had reigned for twenty-one years. No matter ; we have no right, con-
" sidering the scantiness of the information that we possess as to the end
" of the XVIIIth Dynasty, to affirm that Horemheb could not have reigned
" for fifty-nine years. We do not know whether he may have ignored his
" immediate predecessors and dated his reign from the time of the death of
" Amenophis III, counting as his own the years of the reigns of Amenophis IV
" and his short-lived successors."[2]   And he refers to the similar hypothesis
suggested by Petrie à propos of the year 21.   Here, however, the conditions
are no longer the same.   The dates of the year 7, the year 8, and the year
21 have been transmitted to us by documents written under Harmhabi,
whilst that of the year 59 appears amongst pieces collected and copied
under Rameses II, half a century at least after the death of the king.   It is
perhaps conceivable that Egyptian archive keepers may have been commanded
to consider Harmhabi as the immediate successor of Amenôthes III, and, in
fact, it is so on the three tablets of Abydos and Sakkârah, in spite of
the mutilations suffered by the latter: all the years of the heretic king
were set down to Harmhabi, and this king's years were numbered anew,
consecutively, starting from the death of Amenôthes III.   It is less easy
to suppose that he should himself have wrought a sudden change in his
own computation after only a few years.   Manetho's figures are so often
inaccurate or corrupted that we cannot rely upon their testimony against
that which contemporary monuments give us from time to time.   I consider that there is no reason to suspect the date of the year 21.   I would
not say as much for that of the year 59.   It is no doubt possible that
Harmhabi may have reigned for fifty-nine years or more and died almost a
centenarian, like Ramses II ; however, until further light is thrown upon the
subject, I do not see that the general history of the East affords space for
an Egyptian reign of that length.   I am therefore inclined to adopt Loret's
suggestion, as Eduard Meyer[3] has done, or even to propose a yet more
radical solution.   All who have had official functions to perform in modern

---

[1] Flinders Petrie, A History of Egypt, vol. III, pp. 243, 246.
[2] Loret, La Grande Inscription de Mes à Saqqarah, in the Zeitschrift, 1901, vol. XXXIX, p. 4.
[3] Ed. Meyer, Ægyptische Chronologie, p. 90, note 2.

Egypt know with what ease parties in litigations forge *hodjets* and other administrative or legal documents, where land property is concerned, and certain demotic papyri,[1] prove that, in that respect at least, ancient Egyptians did not differ from their descendants. If the contract quoted by Masé should be a forgery of that kind, what would then become of the date of the year 59 ?

We have, therefore, only five certain dates of the reign of Harmhabi, those of the years 1, 3, 7, 8, and 21, and one doubtful one, that of the year 59.

§ V.—THE WARS OF HARMHABI AND HIS ACTIVITY OUTSIDE EGYPT.

Northern Syria had been conquered by the Khati under Khuniatonu, and Egypt no longer had any influence beyond Southern Syria at the time when Harmhabi came into power. We have seen above,[2] on one of the fragments detached from his Memphis tomb, a picture of Asiatic emigrants to the Nile. It is certain that Harmhabi must have turned his attention towards countries which, in his own youth, paid such high tributes to Pharaoh, but no direct traces remain of his activity in that direction, save on one of the Karnak walls, that which connects Harmhabi's two pylons on the east side, and on the last of those pylons. There, on a bas-relief, the princes of the North and the chiefs of the Khati are represented bringing their tributes. The wall, which was brought to light during our excavations in 1882–1883,[3] bears on its southern portion a large picture on which the king is represented bringing to the god Amon a band of prisoners in sufficient numbers to fill three registers of the picture. Between the two upper registers runs a horizontal, half-broken line of hieroglyphs :

"The vile chiefs of the Hauanabu, say : ' Hail to thee ! . . . . has
"spread to the two ends of the world, and thy name is in all countries,
"every land fears thy souls and thy terror is in their hearts.'"

---

[1] See, for instance, the long memoir by Petisis, in Griffith's *Catalogue of the Demotic Papyri in the Rylands Library*, vol. III, pp. 218–250.

[2] See above, pp. 15–18.

[3] Mariette–Maspero, *Monuments Divers*, p. 27.

Thus, in the first register, could be seen the peoples of Asia Minor and of Greece. The second and third contained Syrians in rows of nine and, between the two registers, one horizontal line of inscription :

"The vile princes of . . . . . say : ' Hail to thee ! because (Thy power is) great
". . . . . . (Terror) enters their bowels and Fear is in their hearts.' "

The costume of the figures leaves us no doubt that these were natives of Northern Syria and especially Khati.[1] The list was engraved on the pylon itself, but it has been destroyed, with the exception of eight names which are more or less mutilated :

The names of Khati and Pabukhu prove that the preserved portion of the list belonged to Northern Syria. This convinces me that Max Müller ventured too far when he identified [glyphs] with the Eltekeh of the Bible[3] : this hypothesis would take us too far south. If, on the other hand, we agreed with him in recognizing in [glyphs] the Lullubi, Lullumi, Lullu of Assyrian texts, we should be drawn too far eastwards, into the mountains of Media.[4] It is more likely to be the name of a city or a nation in Cilicia or in the plains of the middle Euphrates. It is not merely probable but almost certain that Harmhabi consolidated or re-established the authority of Egypt over Palestine. But the Hittite documents no longer allow us to suppose that he subdued the Khati and replaced Northern Syria under his

---

[1] The wall has been described and the inscriptions published by Bouriant, *Lettre à M. Max Müller sur le mur d'Horemheb à Karnak*, in the *Recueil de Travaux*, 1895, vol. XVII, pp. 41–44. The line of inscription between the two registers is to be found in Wiedemann, *Texts of the Second Part of the XVIIIth Dynasty*, in the *Proceedings of the Society of Biblical Archæology*, 1889, vol. XI, pp. 423, 424. *Cf.* Breasted, *Ancient Records of Egypt*, vol. III, p. 20.

[2] The list was published by Bouriant, *Lettre à M. Max Müller sur le mur d'Horemheb à Karnak*, in the *Recueil de Travaux*, 1895, vol. XVII, p. 42, and by Max Müller, *Asien und Europa*, p. 292, and *Egyptological Researches*, vol. I, pp. 41, 42, and Pl. 56.

[3] Max Müller, *Egyptological Researches*, vol. I, p. 42, and p. 43, note 3.

[4] Max Müller, *Egyptological Researches*, vol. I, p. 42.

authority. On the contrary, they show that the princes of the Khati continued to occupy the countries which they had torn from the Theban domination during the previous twenty or thirty years, and that they negotiated on equal terms with the Pharaoh. It is even possible that one of the conventions alluded to in the treaty between Ramses and Khaltusîl II was made between Mursîl and Harmhabi.

We are a little better informed as to his doings in the South, against the Puanît and against the negroes of Ethiopia. The tribute of the Puanît is figured on the wall which connects the two Karnak pylons on the north side ; it follows the scene where we see the Asiatics bringing their tribute. Here, however, there is no longer any question of a conquest, for the chiefs of the country are not chained together or bound to the king by the traditional rope, and the scribe does not call them [hieroglyphs] "vile chiefs" but [hieroglyphs] "great chiefs." They have freely renewed their relations with Egypt, interrupted under the heretic Pharaohs, and they are bringing presents to the new sovereign as a sign of friendship rather than submission—gold, gum, and ostrich feathers :

[hieroglyphic text]

"The Great Chiefs of the Puanît say : 'Hail to thee, King of Egypt, Sun of
"the Barbarians of Erythrea, (we swear it) by thy double, we knew not
"Egypt and our fathers had not gone there. Give us of the air that
"thou givest, for all countries are under thy sandals.'"[1]

A second picture, seen almost intact by Champollion[2] but now partly destroyed,[3] represented the king laying before Amon, Maut, and Khonsu the tributes which the chiefs of the tribes of the Puanît had just offered him, especially the gold-dust and precious stones :

[1] The scene was published by Mariette, *Monuments Divers*, Pl. 88, text p. 27 ; the inscription alone by Brugsch, *Recueil de Monuments*, vol. I, Pl. 57, No. 3 ; also by Bouriant, *Lettre à M. Max Müller sur la mur d'Horemheb à Karnak*, in the *Recueil de Travaux*, 1895, vol. XVII, p. 43 ; *cf.* Breasted, *Ancient Records of Egypt*, vol. III, pp. 20, 21.

[2] Champollion, *Monuments de l'Egypte et de la Nubie*, text, vol. I, pp. 180, 181.

[3] Wiedemann, *Texts of the Second Part of the XVIIIth Dynasty*, in the *Proceedings of the Society of Biblical Archæology*, 1889, vol. XI, p. 423, saw a portion of the bas-relief lying at the foot of the wall, and found on it the end of the three, lines more completely copied by Champollion.

"His Majesty causes tributes to be carried to his father Amon, tributes from
"Puanît. (Amon saith : 'Son of my loins, thou hast vanquished all
"nations) by thy valour and strength ; thou hast caused their chiefs to
"be alarmed because of thy terror, (and to come to thee) with all their
"tributes on their backs, for great is thy strength over every foreign
"country.'"

The tribes of the desert, white and black, did not come of their own accord
to render homage, as had been done by those of the Puanît; it was
necessary to reduce them by force, and Harmhabi undertook to lead the
expedition in person. The memory of it has been preserved for us in the
speos of Gebel-Silsileh, not so much the episodes of the campaign as the
triumphant return. In one of the secondary pictures[1] two groups of negroes,
three men and one woman, are gesticulating wildly and crying out in fear at
the approach of the sovereign :

"Princes who were proud in your hearts because you were ignorant of reality,
"say : 'Leap not, O Lion entering into Kaushi.'"

Elsewhere[2] soldiers are seen running, bringing newly-taken prisoners, and
their chief, probably a scribe, salutes Harmhabi :

[1] Champollion, *Monuments de l'Egypte*, Pl. CX ; Rosellini, *Monumenti Storici*, Pl. XLIV
quater ; Lepsius, *Denkmäler*, III, 120 *b*.

[2] Champollion, *Monuments de l'Egypte*, Pl. CXIII ; Rosellini, *Monumenti Storici*, Pl. XLIV
quinquies ; Lepsius, *Denkmäler*, III, Pl. 120 *a* ; *cf*. Brugsch, *Geschichte Ægyptens*, pp. 268, 445,
and Breasted, *Ancient Records of Egypt*, vol. III, p. 22.

[3] The pronoun is omitted here behind the article as it was above (see p. 29, note 2) behind
the verb, in accordance with the vulgar pronunciation.

"Hail to thee, King of Egypt, Sun of the Erythrean Barbarians, thy names
"are great in the land of Kaushi, and thy cry is in their dwellings;
"thy valour, O Excellent Sovereign, changes strange countries into
"heaps of ruins, O Pharaoh, l. h. s., my radiant Shu!"

On the finest bas-relief, that which occupies all the southern part of the western panel, Harmhabi proceeds triumphantly with his victorious troops, in a rich palanquin borne on the shoulders of twelve military chiefs; a high official[1] walks on his left, a fly-whisk in his hand, two chiefs screen him with their long fans, and a priest turns and burns incense before him. The black prisoners march before him in constrained attitudes, to the sound of trumpets, and of boomerangs struck together:

"The good god cometh, he triumphs over the chiefs of all foreign countries
"his bow in his hand, as Ruler of Thebes, the Powerful King who
"reigns, the Most Valiant who brings as prisoners the Chiefs of Kaushi
"the Vile, King of Both Egypts, Zaskhupruriya, Son of the Sun, of
"his loins, Harmhabi Maîamânu, the Vivified. His Majesty returns
"from the land of Kaushi with the prisoners made by his sword, as his
"father Amon had commanded him."

It is the story of one of those raids which the Pharaohs used to make on the tribes of the Upper Nile, almost without any loss in their own troops.

To sum up, if we take into account the few documents which have reached us, it seems that Harmhabi, undisputed ruler of Ethiopia, was able to maintain his supremacy over Southern Syria; the Khati ruled beyond the Thabor and he did not succeed in wrestling their conquests from them.

---

[1] Champollion, *Monuments de l'Egypte*, Pll. CXI–CXIII; Rosellini, *Monumenti Civili*, Pl. XLIV *bis* and *ter*; Lepsius, *Denkmäler*, Pl. 121 *a-b*; *cf.* Champollion, *Lettres écrites d'Egypte*, 1868, pp. 152, 153; Brugsch, *Geschichte Ægyptens*, pp. 445, 446; Breasted, *Ancient Records of Egypt*, vol. III, pp. 21, 22.

§ VI.—THE RESTORATION OF THE CULT OF AMON AND THE CONSTRUCTIONS IN THE TEMPLES.

The inscription of the Turin statue ends by a summary of the measures taken by Harmhabi to restore the temples of the gods as well as their cult, and by a short description of the general joy which they raised in the whole of Egypt :

[hieroglyphic text]

" Now, after was ended this feast at Luxor, and Amonrâsonther had returned
    " in peace to Karnak, His Majesty came down the river as the image of
    " Harmakhuîti and He then ordained this land and organised it as it
    " was in the time of Râ ; He restored the temples of the gods, from the
    " dunes of Adhu to the land of Nubia ; He modelled all their images
    " more numerous than before and more beautiful in their make,[1] so

[1] Lit. : " more numerous than before and more in beauty in what he made of them."

" that the Sun exulted in seeing them, they that had been found in
" ruins in former times ; and He raised up their temple ; He fashioned a
" hundred figures with human bodies according to rule and in all kinds
" of costly stone ; He inspected the cities of the gods which are in the
" districts of this land and He ordained them as they had been since
" the time of creation ; He instituted for them *wakfs* of daily offerings ;
" all the plate for the temples was cast in gold and in silver, and
" he gave them priests, men with scrolls and picked soldiers. He
" assigned to them by authentic deeds cultivated lands and cattle with
" all the necessary material. Therefore do we rise early to sing to the
" Sun in the morning of each day : ' Make long unto us the reign of
" Thy son, who pleaseth Thy heart, Zaskhuprurîya Satpanrîya, and give
" him millions of Royal Jubilees, give him his victories over all lands
" after the example of Horus, son of Isis, because he satisfies thy heart
" in Heliopolis, united as he is to the Ennead of thy gods.' "[1]

The study of the monuments which remain confirms the statements
contained in this inscription. The heretic kings had neglected or ransacked
all the temples of Egypt, even those of which the divinities pleased
them on account of some appearance of affinity with their Atonu : they had
altered the statues and the divine emblems, or they had replaced them by
images which were more than the former in accordance with their philological
concepts. It was in order to repair as far as possible the damage caused by
the introduction into the sanctuaries of these heterodox figures that Harmhabi
caused a hundred figures in human form ⌒🐍 𓀀𓀀 to be made, at the
same time conforming in every point ⌐🪶)| with the prescriptions of the
rituals, and to be cut out of blocks of the most costly stones—red sandstone,
granite, green breccia, and alabaster. The gold and silver plate had in many
cases been taken away or melted to be used for the service of the Solar
Disk; he reconstituted it and, with it, re-established the endowments which
had been turned aside from their legal owners and given to the interloper.
Finally, he had sometimes to renew priesthoods which had been suppressed
or greatly modified. One only of the Theban temples has preserved a
manifest example of this restoration, that of the god Phtah at Karnak.
I have reproduced above the preamble and the date of the inscription

---

[1] Birch, *Inscription of Haremhebi on a Statue of Turin*, Pl. II, lines 21–26; Brugsch,
Thesauraus Inscriptionum Ægyptiacarum, pp. 1077, 1078; *cf.* Breasted, *Ancient Records of
Egypt*, vol. III, pp. 18, 19.

which recorded this fact[1]: it was in the year 1 on the twenty-second day
of the fourth month of Akhaît, only a few weeks after his accession, that
Harmhabi celebrated the feast of the god in the temple and, on this occasion,
instituted a *personnel* composed of seventeen persons : 𓏤𓊹 "the
first prophet of Phtah and Hathor," 𓏤 "the man with the
scroll of Phtah and Hathor," with two assistants entitled [3-4]
" priests of Phtah and Hathor," after whom come a second "man with the
scroll of Phtah and Hathor" (line 5), escorted by three "priests of Phtah and
Hathor" (lines 6–8), a third "man with the scroll" (line 9), with four
"priests" (lines 10–13), and a fourth "man with the scroll" (line 14),
accompanied by three "priests" (lines 15–17). The names have never been
written, and the whole might be a Ptolemaïc restoration, destined to prove
what was the *personnel* of the temple in the time of its splendour. It is
certainly to some similar conception that we owe the stela discovered in 1900
when the temple was cleared. It seemed to me from the first that the
picture which adorns it does not entitle us to affirm that this monument
bears any relation to the restoration of the temple.[2] It is of very fine
workmanship, and represents Harmhabi standing, his helmet on his head,

𓏤 𓏤 followed by 𓏤
𓏤 *Werît Haqaou,* Lady of the Palace, Lady of Heaven, Regent
of all Gods, behind whom a Nile god, wearing his lotus head-dress, is seen
walking, bringing water and flowers on his tray 𓏤
𓏤. The king offers an enormous posy of
flowers to a triad composed of Amonrâsonther 𓏤, who gives him
life, duration, and power according to the formula, 𓏤, of Maut
𓏤, and finally of Khonsu, Good and peaceful in the shape
of a mummy 𓏤. The body of the stela is mutilated, and
perhaps contained some prayer connecting in some way with Phtah the act
performed by the sovereign : for the present we are obliged to confess that
it is not necessarily related to the history of the temple. It is probable
that, at the time of the Ptolemaïc Renaissance, the priests, having found the

[1] See above, pp. 26, 27.

[2] Maspero, *Sur une découverte récente de M. Legrain au temple de Phtah,* in the *Bulletin de l'Institut Egyptien,* 4th series, 1900, vol. I, pp. 81–83, and Legrain, *Le Temple de Phtah-ûs-anbou-f dans Thèbes,* in the *Annales du Service des Antiquités,* vol. III, p. 41.

stela already mutilated and reduced to its present condition in the neighbourhood of their temple, added it to those which they already possessed, and by means of which they were endeavouring to reconstitute their archives.

The other Theban temples are full of bas-reliefs and inscriptions which prove the marvellous activity displayed by Harmhabi in his work of restoration. He built at Karnak the two last southern pylons with fragments from the temple of Atonu.[1] The fine sandstone blocks with which Khouniatonu had built his edifice were broken up and heaped in regular layers; if it were possible to withdraw them without interfering with the solidity of the ruins, we could most probably reconstitute the whole face of the wall. Harmhabi's cartouches are engraved here and there near the sanctuary[2] or in the temple of Khonsu,[3] but what is chiefly striking to a visitor is what remains of the immense avenue of sphinxes which once led from Karnak to Luxor. Were the 128 sphinxes seen by Champollion over eighty years ago[4] all put up by him? All those which still exist in good enough condition for their workmanship to be appreciated resemble each other so absolutely, that it is impossible to doubt that they were carved at the same time by workmen from the same workshops, namely, those of Harmhabi. We have already stated[5] what he did in the great colonnade of Luxor; on the left bank, at Medinet Habou, he repaired the door of one of the chambers of the temple of Hatshopsouîtou and Thoutmôsis III,[6] and he undertook to restore the edifices of Deir el-Baharî.[7] None had suffered more than they from the fanaticism of Khuniatonu; not only had the figures of Amon been hammered out, but also some entire scenes and inscriptions—those on which the queen related the share which the god had had in her birth and in the preliminaries of the expedition to the Puanît. Harmhabi declares that he restored the monument of Thoutmôsis III, father of his fathers,[8] and Petrie judges from the style of the restorations that they were his work for the most part.[9] After an examination on the spot I am inclined to think that

[1] Champollion, *Monuments de l'Egypte et de la Nubie*, text, vol. II, p. 180; Lepsius, *Denkmäler*, III, Pl. 112 *a, b*, 119 *e*.

[2] Champollion, *Monuments de l'Egypte et de la Nubie*, text, vol. II, p. 137.

[3] Champollion, *Monuments de l'Egypte et de la Nubie*, text, vol. II, pp. 217, 221.

[4] Champollion, *Monuments de l'Egypte et de la Nubie*, text, vol. II, p. 174.

[5] See above, p. 23.

[6] Lepsius, *Denkmäler*, III, Pl. 202 *d*.

[7] Champollion, *Monuments de l'Egypte et de la Nubie*, text, vol. I, p. 574; Lepsius, *Denkmäler*, III, Pl. 119 *c*.

[8] Champollion, *Monuments de l'Egypte et de la Nubie*, text, vol. I, p. 574; Lepsius, *Denkmäler*, III, Pl. 119 *c*; see above, p. 7.

[9] Flinders Petrie, *A History of Egypt*, vol. II, p. 254.

Harmhabi did very little at Deir el-Baharî, and that the greater part of the repairs was the work of the early years of Ramses II.

Most of the edifices which he built or rebuilt in Egypt proper have disappeared and left but a few fragments, such as granite capitals[1] and columns from Memphis[2] and an isolated block at Kom Ombo:[3] he seems even to have multiplied his gifts to the Gods of Heliopolis.[4]   Two Apis having died during his reign, Harmhabi buried them in the Serapeum in twin vaults, separated from each other by a wall of stone plastered and painted.[5]   In Nubia, the little speos of Abahuda is fairly well preserved, and its sculptures have very slightly suffered under the paintings with which the Christians of Nubia covered them about the sixth century. They do not tell us anything, unfortunately, concerning the doings of Harmhabi in whose honour they were executed.[6]   The only monument which recalls them is the speos of Silsileh[7]; I have already briefly described the pictures it contains of the raid against the Ethiopians.[8] I pass over a few insignificant stone fragments and come to the fragment discovered by Petrie in 1892, in the temple of Atonu at El-Amarna,[9] and from which he has ventured to deduce some theory as to the ideals which ruled the conduct of the sovereign during the early years of his reign.[10] We have seen above[11] that he adopts for Harmhabi's reign two series of dates beginning the one under Touatânkhamanou, at the time when the latter officially re-established the cult of Amon, the other at the death of Aîya. According to Petrie, the presence of the name of Harmhabi at El-Amarna would prove that, at the beginning, he spared the cult of Atonu and his

---

[1] Wiedemann, *Ægyptische Geschichte*, pp. 409, 410.

[2] They had been carried to Alexandria with the obelisks probably under the Ptolemies, and they were taken to Vienna in the nineteenth century, ARNETH, *Ueber Ægyptische Alterthümer*, in *Sitzungsberichte der K. Akademie zu Wien*, vol. XI ; *cf.* Perrot-Chipiez, *Histoire de l'Art*, vol. I, p. 473.

[3] Legrain, *Notes d'inspection*, § *XLVI*, in *Annales du Service*, 1907, vol. VIII, pp. 57–59.

[4] Prokesch-Osten, *Nilfahrt*, pp. 351, 355 ; *cf.* Wiedemann, *Ægyptische Geschichte*, p. 410. The block has been brought to the Cairo Museum by M. de Morgan.

[5] Mariette, *Sur les soixante quatre Apis*, in the *Bulletin Archéologique de l'Athénæum Français*, 1855, vol. I, p. 53 ; *cf. Œuvres Diverses*, vol. I, pp. 151–158.

[6] Champollion, *Monuments de l'Egypte et de la Nubie*, vol. I, Pl. II, Nos. 1–3, and text, vol. I, pp. 40–42 ; Lepsius, *Denkmäler*, III, Pl. 122 *a-f*.

[7] Champollion, *Monuments de l'Egypte et de la Nubie*, vol. II, Pll. CVIII–CXIII, and text vol. I, pp. 251–261 ; Rosellini, *Monumenti Storici*, Pll. XLIV–XLIV *quinquies* ; Lepsius, *Denkmäler*, III, Pll. 119–121.

[8] See above, pp. 37–39.

[9] Flinders Petrie, *Tell el-Amarna*, Pl. XI, and p. 5.

[10] Flinders Petrie, *A History of Egypt*, vol. II, pp. 246–251.

[11] See above, pp. 33–35.

partisans and even tolerated that his cartouches should be engraved in their temple. This toleration was not prolonged much further than the year 3 of the actual reign, after which Atonu was finally proscribed and disappeared. I think another explanation can be given of the apparently paradoxical fact discovered by Petrie—an explanation more in conformity with the religious customs of Egypt. The heresy of Khuniatonu, in the eyes of the great priesthood of Egypt, consisted in taking a secondary form of a god already known, making a royal residence of the town built in his honour, and attempting to impose him as the god of the whole land, to the detriment of other gods and especially of Amon. After Thebes had again become the capital and Amon the great national god, the heresy died out of its own accord, but Atonu, fallen from his supreme rank, had not lost his place as a local god ; he had remained the ruler of his own city as Amon was ruler of Thebes, and Phtah of Memphis, and thus Harmhabi might, without necessarily showing any special toleration, allow his name to be inscribed in the temple of El-Amarna as he no doubt did in twenty other temples, great and small, in the Nile Valley. In fact, I hold it for certain that he had entirely returned to Amon from the first moment—the tone of the Turin inscription sufficiently proves it—and that he did not need to modify his conduct soon afterwards. The town of Tell el-Amarna was still feebly alive at that time and rendered him the necessary homage by engraving his cartouches on a non-decorated portion of the local sanctuary. If no other king is mentioned in its ruins, the reason is very simple ; it was an artificial creation of one man and had grown to the detriment of Thebes, whose god it temporarily dethroned, and of Hermopolis, which it deprived of half its territory. Immediately the man who had built it died, the religious supremacy returned to Thebes, the usurped territory was given back to Hermopolis, the population scattered, and the town fell back into the condition of a simple village as of yore.

§ VII.—ORDER RESTORED IN THE COUNTRY AND IN THE ADMINISTRATION.

Harmhabi's work as an administrative reformer seems to have been even more considerable than his religious and monumental restorations. All that we know concerning it has been taught us by an enormous stela, of which I discovered the fragments in 1882, in the northern face of the western tower of the southern pylon of Harmhabi at Karnak.[1]   When intact, it was about five metres in height and three metres in breadth; about one-third of its original surface has gone.   The scene which occupied the centre, and which showed us Harmhabi worshipping Amon, only exists in pieces, and the first ten lines are too much destroyed for anything to be understood from them; the loss would not be a great one—since they merely contained the style and panegyric of the prince—if we were sure that no date was to be found. The main part of the document consisted of thirty-nine horizontal lines, and the last words went over the sides.   Copied, published, and analysed by Bouriant, with mistakes rendered excusable by its lamentable state when first discovered,[2] discussed and translated from Bouriant's text,[3] then copied and published a second time by Max Müller,[4] and then, after the drying and removal of the sticky mud which plastered the surface had rendered legible a great number of groups and letters invisible or indistinct at first, it was translated anew by Breasted[5] from an unpublished copy of Gardiner's.

The preamble, which begins with line 9, tells us that the king wished but "to render justice to both lands in Egypt, and rejoiced to exalt their beauty," and then proceeds to show him deliberately pondering over the best means of restoring them[6]:

---

[1] Maspero, *Notes sur quelques points de Grammaire et d'Histoire*, in the *Zeitschrift*, 1882, vol. XX, p. 134.

[2] Bouriant, *A Thèbes*, in the *Recueil de Travaux*, vol. VI, pp. 41–46.

[3] W. Max Müller, *Erklärung des grossen Dekrets des Königs Har-em-hebe*, in the *Zeitschrift*, 1888, vol. XXVI, pp. 70–94.   A French translation was published by Révillout in the *Revue Egyptologique*, vol. VIII, pp. 129–139, entitled *Les réformes et les rêves d'un roi philanthrope*.

[4] W. Max Müller, *Egyptological Researches*, vol. I, pp. 56–59, and Pll. 90–104.

[5] Breasted, *Ancient Records of Egypt*, vol. III, pp. 22–33.

[6] About two-thirds of each line are missing.

" His Majesty took counsel with his own heart . . . . . . (and found what it was
" fitting to do in order to) destroy sin and to annihilate falsehood.
" Now the counsels of His Majesty are as a perfect refuge which repulses
" violence from Kamî . . . . . . (and his thoughts are a bulwark which
" protects the people from the evils) which exist within, for, behold,
" His Majesty watches by day and by night, seeking the utility of Egypt
" and investigating the acts (of violence which are committed in the
" country) . . . . . . (He therefore called the scribe of) His Majesty ; the
" latter therefore seized the palette and the scroll of papyrus and put
" down in writing all that His Majesty said ; The King himself spoke,
" saying : ' (My Majesty) orders . . . . . . (that it shall be done as follows
" against) the acts of violence which are committed in the country.' "

It is, in fact, a collection of decrees, which are arranged according to the
nature of the offences mentioned. The first four state the penalties to be
inflicted on officials or soldiers guilty of taking from peasants, for their own
use, any duty in kind which the latter might have set aside for the royal
mansion :

"If the villein has procured for himself a barque with its sail in order to
"serve Pharaoh, l. h. s. . . . . . (and to deliver unto Him his dues
"destined to the breweries and kitchens[1] of Pharaoh, l. h. s., if the
"villein is robbed of this barque with his) dues, and if he should thus
"remain despoiled of his goods and deprived (of the fruit) of his labours,
"(that is not good, that goes against what My Majesty has ordered in)
"his excellent measures.   If therefore he who pays his dues, destined to
"the breweries and kitchens (of the palace,) to the two *wékils* (of the
"army remains despoiled of his goods, My Majesty orders that any
"individual whatsoever who has stolen those dues) and has violently
"seized upon the boat of any denizen, military or civilian, who is in the
"whole land, he will suffer the application of the law by the ablation of
"his nose, and by relegation to Zaru.[2]   (II. Item, concerning the wood-
"dues, if a royal officer finds) a villein who has no boat, let him bring to
"that villein a boat ordered from another for his service, and let him
"despatch that other promptly to bring the wood of the villein, for
"he is in the service (of the king.   III. Item, if the boat of a poor
"man be seized vio)lently and it be despoiled of his cargo by robbery,
"so that the poor man remains despoiled of his (goods, no other due
"will be exacted from him since) he has nothing left, for it would not
"be right, and this affair would be an act of extreme iniquity.   My
"Majesty orders that he be exonerated and behold . . . . . . (IV. Item,
"concerning those who tow[3] for the Royal House), and those who tow
"them for the Harem and also for the offerings to all the gods, paying
"their dues to the two *wékils* of the army, and . . . . . . (If some one

---

[1] The conjunction of these two departments, now always so far apart, was only natural in
Egypt.   The bas-reliefs of the Memphis mastabas and the scenes enacted by wooden dolls in the
tombs of the Heracleopolitan and first Theban periods, represent them next to each other;
cooks, grain-grinders, bakers, brewers, and butchers are constantly seen together.   As barley
fermentation was obtained by means of bread-crumbs used as yeast, the vicinity of the brewery
and kitchens, or rather of the *places* where not only meats but also bread and pastry
were prepared was almost a necessity.

[2] Zaru, Sellé, on the eastern frontier of Egypt, chief town of the XIVth Nome of the Delta.

[3] probably means *drawing with a rope*, and applies to a boat or a sleigh, then by
an extension of the term, to an image, a linen chest, provisions, etc., carried on a barrow.
Here the word is opposed to , which signifies to carry by means of a sailing barque
which does not require towing with a rope.

" should rob him, My Majesty commands) that he should suffer the
" application of the law by the ablation of his nose and by relegation to
" Zaru in retaliation."

The object of these four decrees, which supported and completed each
other, was to ensure the regular working of the service of supply for the
royal table, for the harem and for the temples, by preventing provisions
of solid or liquid food and wood intended for the kitchens from being stolen,
between the time when they were sent off by the tax-payer and that when
they should reach the store-houses of Pharaoh, of the harem, or of the gods.
These contributions in kind travelled either on sailing ships ⸻
⸻ or on sailless barges towed with ropes, or carried on men's
shoulders or animals' backs ⸻. Two of these orders relate to the
punishment of the robbers by ablation of the nose and relegation to a
frontier town ; the two others are intended to assist the robbed tax-payer by
the loan of a barque, or to compensate him for his loss by declaring that he
should not have to replace the stolen dues.

The two following articles appear to refer to some requisitions for slaves or
other valuables falsely made in the name of the sovereign in the private
interest of some civil or military authorities :

"When the auditors of the store-house of Pharaoh, l. h. s., go into the
"town to collect the tax (of safflower, if, as they go from house to house,
"they seize upon the slaves of the villein) during six days or during
"seven days so that one cannot make use of them[1] as that is an awful
"manner (of behaving), let the same be done (unto the auditors).
"Therefore then, when in any place (where the auditors of the
"store-house of Pharaoh, l. h. s., shall go it shall) be heard said: 'They
"are collecting the safflower-tax,' and afterwards someone else shall
"come to report: 'My slave has been seized upon, or my (handmaid,
"during six days or during seven days, so that I could not make use
"of them,' let the same be done to the auditors.)[2]   VI. (Now) the
"two divisions of soldiers, one in the region of the South, the other in
"the region of the North, stole the skins of oxen in the whole land,
"without leaving a year's respite so that (the people) should have rest,
"(but they came, under pretext of taking) count (of the registered oxen)
"and of taking from the people the oxen marked (with the royal seal)
"and, going from house to house, they beat and plundered, so that no
"skins were left (for the peasants); (on the other hand) when (the
"steward of the oxen) of Pharaoh, l. h. s., came (to register the oxen)
"in fact and to (take away the skins of the dead oxen) . . . . . . he

---

[1] Lit.: "without that one can go with them for an expedition."
[2] Lit.: "let it be done in duplicate, in the same manner," which I interpret by an application
of the law of talion: "the comptrollers having harmed the peasants, let harm be done unto them."

" found no skins with the peasants, though their arrears (of dues) could
" be stated against them, and they were content to say[1] : 'The skins
" have been stolen from us ;' as (those thefts) constitute a villany, let
" the same be done to the robbers. Therefore, when the steward of the
" oxen of Pharaoh, l. h. s., comes to register the oxen in the whole land,
" and to take away the skins of the dead oxen which (form Pharaoh's
" due, he will exempt the peasants robbed in this way) in his spirit
" of equity, and (on the other hand) any individual of the soldiery
" of whom it shall be heard said : 'He comes to take away the skins,'
" from that day let him come under the law by a flogging of a hundred
" strokes, with five open sores and by confiscation of the skin which he
" violently took from the peasant."

The bond between these two orders only becomes clear if we suppose that
the plant called *kata* ⊔ 🐭 ᵒ, of which the seeds and flowers were utilised
by the Egyptians, was safflower or some plant used for dyeing purposes : the
theft of the plant hindered the industry of dyed leather, and the theft of the
leather rendered useless the cultivation of the plant. If the soldiery is
particularly mentioned in connection with the skins of oxen, it is because a
considerable quantity of leather was required for their bucklers, quivers, etc.
The mention of the dead oxen and of the officials entrusted with the
registration of royal cattle is explained by a custom stiil very usual in
modern Oriental administration : when something is broken or when an
animal dies, he who had charge of it is bound to produce the fragments or
the skin, without which he has to replace the article or the animal at his
own expense. When the steward of the oxen of Pharaoh went to make his
census ⌂ 🦊 ⫶ and to renew the registration of the cattle in the peasants'
hands, the latter were bound to produce the skins of the dead oxen and, the
soldiers having stolen them, they could not do so. Harmhabi apparently
decided that they should not be compelled to give more skins for the store-
house, and severely punished the guilty parties :

---

[1] Lit. : " having known to establish the remnants against them, they *filled their hearts*,
saying :"

8.

[hieroglyphic text]

This seventh paragraph is so much mutilated that I cannot be certain of having arrived at the complete meaning of it. It dealt with another kind of abuse which was

> " (committed by the officers who had to levy the toll on the ships which
> " came down and went up the river) to the land, and which took place
> " (when the scribes of the table) of the queen's house, and the scribes
> " of the table of the harem were set on the tracks of the officers
> " (entrusted with the levying of this toll), to repress and to enquire into the
> " affair of the toll on the ships which went upstream and downstream."

It seems to me that we have here a mention of facts connected with two different classes of institutions. The Oriental princes were in the habit of allocating to their queens, and, in general, to the women of their family, the revenues of a special town or the product of certain taxes : · if I am not mistaken, here, the intervention of the scribes of the table of the queen's house and of the two harems proves that the right of toll levied in certain places, on the ships which went up or came down the Nile, was assigned to the food supply of the women. Under the Ptolemies, this toll was exacted at the frontier of the nome of Aphroditopolis and of the nome of Hermopolis, at the *Theban Watch* and at the *Hermopolitan Watch ;* customs endure so long in Egypt that I should not be surprised if it had been so in anterior times. However it may have been, these navigation dues on upstream and down-stream traffic [hieroglyphs] gave rise to old-established abuses on the part of those who had charge of it.

> " Enquiries had been directed on the subject against the customs officers
> " under King Manakhpirrîya ; for, as to the dues[1] on navigation which
> " were exacted since (the officers of the queen's house at the time
> " of King) Manakhpirrîya were set on the tracks of (those officers) every
> " year, (when the peasants made) the expedition to Thebes,[2] and since
> " the officers of the double harem went to these officers saying : ' Cause
> " the expedition to be suspended,' behold, Pharaoh caused the expedition
> " of the feast at Karnak to take place every year, without interruption,
> " and, since then, are placed before His Majesty, l. h. s., (the goods with
> " which the barques are laden)."

It seems to me that at a given moment the scribes of the table had plotted with the toll-gatherers to oblige the ships which brought a cargo to Thebes for the fair, which took place annually in that city at the time of the feast of Amon,[3] to stop on their way and suspend their journey [hieroglyphs]. This may have been intended to force the peasants to pay some backsheesh, in order to hasten the formalities connected with the toll, or to allow the officials to buy for next to nothing, or even to confiscate, goods arriving too late for the fair, but this is a mere hypothesis. All we know is that Pharaoh had taken the matter in hand, and that henceforward the ships arrived in good time for the feast without being stopped on the way [hieroglyphs]. As to the means by which he obtained this result, and the penalties which he enacted against the delinquents, I cannot succeed in deciphering them.

Paragraphs VIII and IX are even more damaged than the preceding one. I can only make out from them, the same as Max Müller, that they dealt with robberies of forage committed by underlings in Pharaoh's pantries at the expense of the peasants, the latter being despoiled of their forage under

---

[1] Lit.: " the dues on navigation which a [hieroglyphs] (?) levied [hieroglyphs]." [hieroglyphs] is the technical word from which was derived the name given by the Egyptians to the inland customs, and transcribed Σχεδια by the Greeks whence the Abschadé ([Coptic]) of modern maps.

[2] [hieroglyphs], lit.: " to the town *par excellence,*" which at that time was Thebes.

[3] See above, pp. 23 *sqq.*

pretence of collecting the tax, after which the real tax-gatherers came to claim
Pharaoh's dues, so that the peasants were compelled to pay a second time.[1]
It is better to pass on to the texts engraved on the left section of the
monument, in which Harmhabi relates in an emphatic but nevertheless
interesting manner what he did to reorganise Egypt,[2] how he consolidated
the whole land, travelling along it in a ship in order to become acquainted
with its whole extent, and thoroughly explored every corner.   He

> " chose men of finished elocution, endowed with excellent qualities, clever
> " in judging the depths of bosoms, respectful of the words of the Royal
> " Palace and of the laws of the tribunals ; I installed them solemnly to
> " judge over both countries ; . . . . (I placed them each in) his place,
> " and I placed them in the great cities of the South and of the North,[3]
> " and the whole country comes to one of them without exception, for I
> " have given them my instructions (which are inscribed as) laws in the
> " diary (of the palace) . . . . I have directed them straight in the way
> " of life, I have guided them towards Justice and I have instructed them
> " saying : 'Do not fraternise with the vulgar, receive no presents from
> " others.' . . . . For every officer, Prophet of the God, of whom it shall
> " be heard said : 'He, who sits to render justice among the council
> " chosen for judgments, he sins against justice,' this shall be to him a
> " crime worthy of death.   And My Majesty acted in this manner in
> " order to perfect the laws of Egypt . . . . I constituted the body of the
> " divine fathers and prophets of the temples, of the officers of the palace
> " of this country, also of the priests of the gods who complete this body,
> " so that they may judge the inhabitants of all towns, for My Majesty
> " rises early over Egypt in order that should prosper the life of her
> " inhabitants when My Majesty rises on the throne of Râ.   Certainly
> " since the body has been established for the whole land, all its
> " members will constitute a judicial body according to the perfect
> " designs (of My Majesty)."

[1] W. Max Müller, *Erklärung des grossen Dekrets des Königs Har-em-hebe*, in the *Zeitschrift*,
1886, vol. XXVI, pp. 73–75, 88, 89 ; *cf.* Breasted, *Ancient Records of Egypt*, vol. III,
pp. 29, 30.

[2] Max Müller, *Egyptological Researches*, vol. I, Pl. 99, 102, and *Zeitschrift*, 1886, vol. XXII,
pp. 73, 74 ; *cf.* Breasted, *Ancient Records of Egypt*, vol. III, pp. 31–33.

[3] Gardiner reads here [hieroglyphs] instead of [hieroglyphs], which is marked as doubtful in Müller's
text ; he concludes from it that the judicial body was identical with the two supreme courts
which depended on the Prime Minister under Thoutmôsis III (*The Inscription of Més*, p. 34).
The return of [hieroglyphs] in the plural on line 7 leads me to prefer Müller's reading.

It was a complete restoration of the judiciary organisation which had been greatly compromised during the disturbances which had followed the reform of Amenôthes IV. Harmhabi, after describing it, ends the inscription by relating how he treated the soldiers who watched over him in his palace :

" They kept watch around him $\left(\begin{array}{c}\end{array} \right)$ the space of one month, then he
  " offered them a sort of feast at which each man sat before a portion
  " of all that was good, bread, meats, and cakes from the stores of the
  " king's palace . . . . ."

Their joy at this boon was noisily displayed :

  " voices reached unto Heaven, praising the beauties of their Ruler ; all
  " the heads of the militia, all the chiefs of the soldiers, every man
  " manifested his delight. My Majesty appeared unto them, throwing
  " them gifts from a balcony, even calling each man by his name. They
  " sally forth before him in rejoicing, laden with provisions from the
  " royal palace, for, certainly they received masses of corn from the
  " granary, each of them, barley and millet, and not one of them was
  " found to have none of it . . . ."

Afterwards they returned

  " to their cities, not having completed in the Residence their days of
  " service $\left(\begin{array}{c}\end{array} \right)$, but their sergeants ran behind them
  " as far as their living place,"

to see them to their homes. The text ends with this curious indication, Harmhabi, carried to the throne by the soldiery, and having had to repress the excesses which they committed, nevertheless took care to preserve his authority over them by dealing out abundant largesse, and by shortening the time of service for each section of the army which came in rotation to keep watch over his palace.

It is a pity that such an important document should not have been better preserved. Such as it is, and in spite of its lacunæ, it allows us to appreciate fairly exactly what may be called the legislative work of Harmhabi. Egypt was very unsettled at the time of his accession, and the state of disorganisation from which the country suffered was no doubt chiefly due to himself. Though in the Turin inscription he represented his advent to the throne as a normal fact, accomplished peacefully under the inspiration of Amon, it is probable that the support of the army materially assisted the divine will; the disorders which he attempted to reform were due to his own ambition as much as to the tenacity of the partisans of the Atonian reform, and he merely endeavoured to heal wounds that he had previously made. Moreover, the abuses which he tried to remedy were chiefly of a kind which tended to affect his own income. It was because the skins and provisions intended for the royal household no longer reached their destination, and he and his harem suffered in consequence, that he pronounced penalties against the civil or military officials who intercepted the goods for their own profit. Certainly the general interests of justice were not indifferent to him, but they came after his private interests, and were only taken into consideration in connection with the latter. This is less a personal characteristic of Harmhabi than a consequence of the political constitution of Egypt under the second Theban empire. Pharaoh was sole ruler of the soil; he and he alone was really the State. It was necessary for the good of his person that Egypt should be prosperous, and that the people should be well administered. If he could have separated his own destiny from that of his subjects, he would certainly have given little thought or trouble to the security of their persons and property; as he depended upon them for the services which they rendered him, he was constrained to take the best care he could of them and therefore of his own necessities. Harmhabi, though he may not have treated them as the modern concept of royalty would require that he should, behaved equitably according to the ideas which ruled the world in his time. If he showed as much decision in the execution of his decrees as he had done in the enacting of them, he deserves to be classed among the good sovereigns of Egypt.

Not to speak here of such steles of Touatânkhamanou on which he inscribed his name,[1] he has left in all the land traces of his activity, from the districts near the Second Cataract down to the Delta,[2] and two Apis bulls having died

---

[1] For instance the large stele found at Karnak, and which is now in the Cairo Museum (Legrain, *Notes d'Inspection,* § *XXVII*, in *Annales du Service*, 1905, t. VI, p. 192, and *la Grande Stele de Tutankhamanou à Karnak*, in *Recueil de Travaux*, 1907, t. XXIX, pp. 162–173); see above, pp. 23, 27.

[2] Wiedemann gives a list of all the monuments bearing the name of Harmhabi or dating from his reign which were known in 1884–1888 (*Ægyptische Geschichte*, pp. 408–418, and *Supplement*, pp. 47, 48). Their number has not increased much since then; however, we may quote the great stele from Heliopolis which Daressy found in Cairo for our Museum (*Inscriptions hiéroglyphiques trouvés dans le Caire*, in *Annales du Service*, t. IV, pp. 105–106), the statue of Maia, the Theban sculptor (Legrain, *Notes d'Inspection,* § V, in *Annales du Service*, t. IV, pp. 213–218), the Dattari fragmentary stele in the Cairo Museum (Legrain, *Notes d'Inspection,* § XLVI, in *Annales*, t. VIII, pp. 57–59).

in his days, he buried them at Sakkarah.[1] We may, therefore, believe that his reign was happy at home and of fairly long duration. We have seen above[2] that the last certain date is that of the year 21 : it is impossible at present to know how long he reigned afterwards. The lists of Manetho,[3] which sometimes assign to him four years and one month, sometimes five years, and sometimes nine years, have no value in this connection, and all the explanations of these figures which have been given rest on very uncertain combinations. It is not known under what circumstances he died, nor whether he left any children. His tomb remained unfinished. Ramses I, who succeeded him, does not seem to have been directly connected with him in any way. Is there some truth in the tradition according to which he was ejected from his throne? The other tradition which introduces his name into the legend of Danaos may date from a somewhat distant epoch, but, under its present form, it too evidently belongs to the cycle of romantic fancies by means of which Alexandrinian scholars endeavoured to connect the heroic times of Grecian history with the history of Egypt, for us to be entitled to accept the smallest particle of it. It is better to put it entirely aside and to rely on the sole testimony of contemporary monuments ; after consulting this, we are obliged to confess that Harmhabi disappears from the stage as mysteriously as he appeared on it.

[1] See above, p. 44.
[2] See above, pp. 31–33.
[3] Unger, *Manetho*, p. 158.

LUXOR,
12th January, 1911.

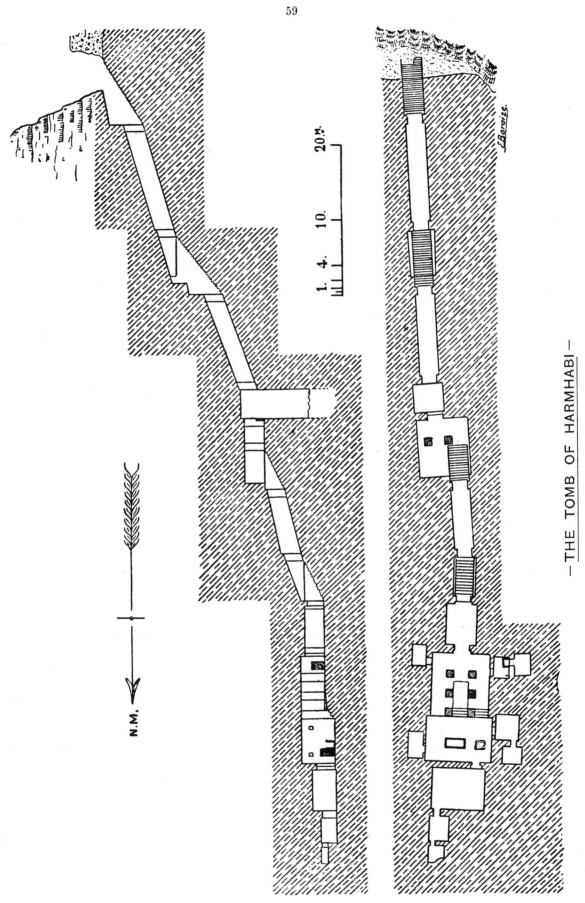

20 M.

10.

4.

1.

N.M.

E.Barois.

—THE TOMB OF HARMHABI—

III.

INSCRIPTIONS AND DECORATION OF THE TOMB OF HARMHABI.

BY SIR GASTON MASPERO.

THE plan and general arrangement of the tomb of Harmhabi are practically the same as we find in the royal hypogea of the XIXth Dynasty, in that of Setuî I, for instance; the tomb, however, has been left unfinished, and it is possible that some of its parts, where the walls are bare, such as the entrance passage, were not intended to be decorated.

Only three of the rooms have received the customary ornamentation of paintings and sculpture: the room of the well, the room which leads into the Golden Hall and the Golden Hall itself; many of the subjects on the walls of this last are mere sketches. It is everywhere apparent that the work, begun at leisure with scrupulous care, was suddenly interrupted. The death of the prince, as usual, caused it to be left as it was at the moment, and the workmen retired in haste to make room for the priests and such other persons as were concerned in the funeral ceremony. As I have already had occasion to note of the Memphitic Age, in the pyramid of Ouanas, they did not trouble to remove the stone splinters and the débris of all kinds which cumbered the ground. It seemed to me, after examination, that a gangway had been cleared across the rooms in order to make the access to the sarcophagus easy for the bearers of the mummy and of the offerings. The well room and the room in front of the Golden Hall are almost perfect, the scenes having been carved and afterwards painted. The door which leads from the descending passage to the well room, and that which opens from it into the ante-room, had been walled up, but they were dismantled afterwards on the right side by the robbers, thus causing the disappearance of figures already finished; except for that, the decoration is intact and as fresh as if it had just left the craftsman's hands. The Golden Hall was being decorated when the king died: the picture nearest to the eastern door is partly painted, but the eyes of most of the figures are left blank; the two scenes which covered the east and west walls were drawn in ink and then corrected by the head limner, and the sculptor had begun his work on some of them, as can be seen on Pll. XLVII–L, LVI–LX. In that part of the Golden Hall which was reserved for the sarcophagus, only the picture of the Judgment is

10.

correctly drawn ; the others are barely begun, and in fact the wall which was to receive them is merely divided into the three customary registers. As each subject had its special place, according to that which it was believed to have once had in the *Hidden House of Horus*, the head limner had traced on the walls some marks for the guidance of his workmen ; some of these marks can be seen distinctly on our Pll. LII–LIII, ⸗ north, ⸗, ⸗ and ⸗ west, ⸗ north-east, and on the pillar facing the sarcophagus the somewhat mysterious indication ⸗ " Southern façade of the land of the Anou (?)."

This unfinished condition, which is deplorable in many ways, allows us to ascertain the exact methods of the Egyptian decorator. As soon as the stonemason had completed his work, one of the draughtsmen began to transfer from his book of designs to the wall the subjects chosen for the decoration. He first divided the space into as many horizontal compartments as there were registers to be reproduced, three in this instance, carefully reserving along the top a space more or less wide, according as to whether the scene was surmounted by a row of ⸗ *khakerû*, or defined by a mere band ; all along the bottom he reserved a dado of variable height. He then rapidly sketched the figures and inscriptions in each register, first drawing straight horizontal lines along the whole length of the register to ascertain the positions of the heads of the standing personages and of certain accessories such as the tow-ropes, which practically marked the middle of the human bodies. Then, by means of lines drawn or merely indicated perpendicularly across the horizontal lines, he divided it into as many equal compartments as there were similar figures of a given length, and he surrounded each of those figures by a rapid outline. For the legends, he drew down from the upper line of the register as many vertical lines as there were columns of writing in his pattern-book. Sometimes it happened that the latter was in bad condition and that a hole in the papyrus or a scratch on the wooden tablet which bore it had removed several signs ; he then left in each column a blank to correspond roughly with the number of signs which were missing, and he inscribed a note in hieratic characters explaining that here was a lacuna, ⸗ "found empty." When he had done, a headman came, who rectified the position and attitude of the figures, carefully drew the hieroglyphs and carried the execution so far that the sculptor had only to follow automatically the outlines thus prepared for him. Where the relief was to be flat the line was neat and even from one end to the other ; where a light modelling was required to connect the contour with the raised parts of the figure, as is the case with the bullocks, the draughtsman indicated by a slight tint the surfaces to be modelled. However great his skill, that of the sculptor who assisted him was no less remarkable ; it is impossible to imagine more firmness together with more suppleness than they showed in carving the stone, more delicacy of touch or more scientific gradation of effect.

Our first impression on entering these rooms is one of unmitigated admiration. The colours are still so fresh, the play of tones so harmonious though so bright, the arrangement of the figures on the walls is so well balanced that we can feel nothing but pleasure and satisfaction. However, when we pass from a mere glance at the whole to a study of every detail we cannot but discover certain faults which had passed unnoticed at first. There is stiffness in the bodies, the heads are long and heavy, the figures are lacking in life : it is the work of an admirable workman rather than that of an artist. Certainly Harmhabi cannot have chosen for the decoration of his own tomb the least good among the *personnel* of the royal workshops at Thebes, and, on the other hand, some bas-reliefs at Luxor and Karnak show that he had at his disposal many a true artist, free from the faults which we are fain to recognise in the decorators of his tomb. Are we to conclude that, in consequence of the religious troubles, the royal workshops of Thebes had suffered and no longer counted a sufficient number of skilled masters to work at the same time both for the temples and for the tombs ? When we pass from the hypogeum of the tomb of Harmhabi to that of Setuî I, we cannot but observe how like they are in design, and at the same time how much more perfect the sculptures of the former are than those of the latter. Hardly a quarter of a century had elapsed between the two, and it is probable that a few of the artists who had been employed for Harmhabi were employed again for Setuî, at least when the work began. This is but an hypothesis ; what is certain is that the affinity between the handiwork of the one and that of the other is such that we must acknowledge them to be the work, if not of the same hands, at least of the same school. It would seem that Setuî divided the body of sculptors trained under Harmhabi into two groups, one of which was sent to Abydos to work at the two Memnonia, whilst the other remained at Thebes, decorated the tombs of Ramses II, of Menephtah, and of Setuî II, with some parts of Gournah, and disappeared or completely altered its style during the latter years of the XIXth Dynasty.

The decoration of the first two rooms includes merely such commonplace scenes of worship that there is no necessity to transcribe and to translate the texts : they can easily be read on the Plates in this book. This is not the case with the scenes figured in the Golden Hall ; the superposition of the finished design over the sketch has sometimes blurred the characters in such a way as to make the texts difficult to read on the Plates. I have therefore interpolated them in the body of this work in order to make them more easy to study.

DECORATED WELL ROOM.

(Plates XXV–XXX.)

Originally, the Southern door beyond the well was barred by a wall which was painted over, so that intruders coming into the tomb should believe that the well marked the end of the passages. The thieves, who were perfectly aware of this, were not deceived by it; they broke the wall and thus destroyed part of the pictures. Two series of these run parallel to each other, west and east, on the walls of this room. The king, represented living, is seen alternately offering the four-fold homage or presenting wine to the divinities whom he must conciliate in order to obtain a favourable reception in the other world, i.e., Osiris as a mummy and his two sisters Isis and Hathor, Harsiesi, Anubis and Naftâmou 𓊪𓈖𓏏𓁹 . He goes from one to the other, receiving their welcome and their gifts, until he reaches the extremity of the hall.

Western Series.

(Plates XXV–XXVI.)

South-West Wall.—On the small panel which covers this wall a black jackal is represented, a collar on his neck and a whip on his back, stretched on a pedestal which is like the façade of a tomb 𓉐, "Anubis, Chief of the Divine Tent" (⟵) 𓇋𓈖𓊪𓅱�𓏏, "Great God on his mountain, Ruler of the Augarît."

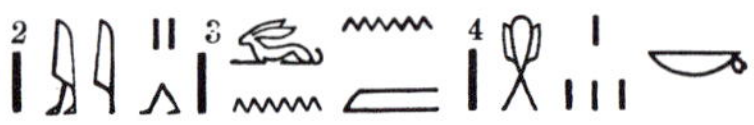

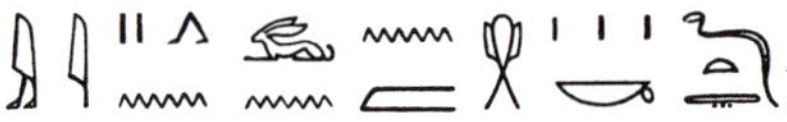

West Wall.—Harsiesi, falcon-headed, wearing the pskhent, holds the king by the hand and leads him to his mother Isis, who wears on her head the two cow's horns and the solar disk. Horus says : (⟶) 𓎼𓂝𓈖𓏤𓁹� "I come to be thy protector, I have composed "for thee thy flesh, and I have given thee the throne of Osiris." Isis, in her turn, repeats that : (⟵) 𓇋𓏤𓈖𓈖� "I come to be thy "protectress eternally," and says that she "came to him in order that he "should be in heaven like Râ"; she adds : [hieroglyphs] "thou "becomest my brother, Ruler of both lands." So, after being presented to Isis, he may be seen offering wine (⟶) [hieroglyphs] to the goddess Hathor who lives in Thebes, Regent of the Western Mountain, who bears on her head the sign [hieroglyph] of the West. Having won with his offering the good-will of the goddess, Harmhabi enters before the mummy of Osiris and worships it four times in order that it may vouchsafe unto him the gift of life (⟶) [hieroglyphs].

North-West Wall.—The western part of the wall which closed the door has disappeared ; we can only trace out, near the corner, the remnants of a Horus with a human body and a falcon's head, wearing the pskhent, and beside Horus fragments of a legend. The wall has been cut down by the robbers and the scene destroyed in order to widen the door.

Eastern Series.

(*Plates* XXVII–XXX.)

South-East Wall.—The king, entering the room in full royal costume, is received by Harsiesi, the falcon-headed, and by Hathor of the funeral mountain [hieroglyphs], bearing on her head the sign [hieroglyph] of the West ; she seizes him by the hand to lead him on his way. Here the principal speech is addressed to him by Horus : (⟶) [hieroglyphs] "I have placed thy name in the writings, and thy heart is joyful in "the Augarît."

East Wall.—Harsiesi, the falcon-headed, wearer of the pskhent, introduces the Pharaoh to Isis his mother, who greets him twice, first in the short legend which runs from the mouth of the goddess to that of the king : (⟶) [hieroglyphs] "I come to thee, Ruler of Both Lands"; secondly in the three-line inscription which is traced above his head : (⟶) [hieroglyphs] (sic) [hieroglyphs] "I come to thee, my beloved son, and I have "given thee the throne of Osiris in order that thou shouldst rest (*bis*)." From Isis, Harmhabi passes on to Hathor, who resides in Thebes, Lady of Heaven, Regent of all the Gods, who protects her son, Ruler of Both Lands (⟶) [hieroglyphs]; he offers her the wine in the two ritual vases [hieroglyph], *namsat*, (⟶) [hieroglyphs]; and he stops in front of Osiris the mummy, who is crowned with the diadem *Iatef*, and whose hands are armed with the whip /\ and the crook ? , Osiris-Ounnofri Great God ⸺ "King of the Living." He remains standing before him, his arms hanging down, whilst the god greets him as being his son Horus the Most Wise ⸺ .

North-East Wall.—The part of the wall which masked the bay of the door was destroyed, and the greater part of the picture painted on it was taken away when the thieves entered the tomb. The king's figure then disappeared, and nothing remains of it but part of a tray laden with offerings, with the edge of the white tunic and the point of the right foot. The gods are well preserved : (1) Osiris (the mummy) crowned with the diadem *Iatef*, the key of life, and the crook in his hands, is seated on his throne, and, behind him, (2) Anubis, a jackal's head on a man's body, lays his hand on his neck in order to infuse the life-power, the ⸺ *sa*, into him; (3) Horus, falcon-headed. The titles of Osiris run thus : " Osiris, Great God, " Everlasting Ruler, Ounnofri, Ruler of Heaven ; " Anubis is " Anupu, in Ouît, " the city of the funereal vest, Great God, Who is on this mountain, Who " resides in the land of Augarît," the necropolis of his earthly city. Osiris welcomes the king in kindly words :

" I come to thee, to strengthen thy name, both hands in unction on thy " face, in order that thou shouldst be in heaven like Râ, that thou shouldst " rise whole, and that thou shouldst be powerful (*bis*), Ruler of both lands."

ROOM IN FRONT OF THE GOLDEN HALL.

(PLATES XXXI–XL.)

The double series of pictures continue symmetrically on each side of this room, describing the progress made by the king towards the Golden Hall.

WESTERN SERIES.

(*Plates* XXXI–XXXIV.)

South-West Wall.—The king is received and embraced by Hathor, Who resides in Thebes ⸺ ; she wears on her head the sign ⸺ of the West.

West Wall.—Harmhabi, of the True Voice under Osiris-Khontamentît, stands alone in front of Anubis, Head of the Divine Hall, he of the jackal's head on a man's body, who comes towards him to be his protector; he then offers the two vessels of wine to Isis the Great, Regent of Both Lands, wearing the two horns and the solar disk. Thence he goes into the presence of Harsiesi of the Hawk's head and worships him four times according to custom; afterwards he passes on to Hathor Who resides in Thebes and he offers her the two flasks of wine. The last picture represents him in a fourfold act of adoration before Osiris-Khontamentît.

North-West Wall.—All the portion in the neighbourhood of the door is broken. In the angle we can see the remnants of a figure of the king presenting the perfumed unguent ☖ to a Phtah-Sokaris (mummy) standing against a great 𝍖 *didu*, the same size as the buckle 𝍕 of the opposite panel.

Two pictures are inscribed in the opening of the door leading to the Golden Hall, and they represent the goddess Maât, her feather ⸢𝍐⸣ on her head. She is standing with her face turned to the east, and seems to be awaiting the sovereign in order to lead him into his vault.

EASTERN SERIES.

(*Plates* XXXV–XL.)

South-East Wall.—On the narrow panel which occupies the whole of this wall, Harmhabi is welcomed by Harsiesi, wearing the pskhent on his hawk's-head, and Hathor, Residing in Thebes ⸢𝍖⸣, Lady of Heaven, Regent of the Gods, crowned with the sign 𝍔 of the West.

East Wall.—Having been introduced, Harmhabi makes an offering of wine to Anubis, Ruler of the Necropolis ⸢𝍖⸣, he of the human body and the jackal's head, and the latter welcomes him with the common-place formula (➡) ⸢𝍖⸣ "I am come to thee, Son of My Body, Well Beloved," which is repeated a little lower down on the vertical column which runs down alongside the jambs, with the addition: (➡) ⸢𝍖⸣ "I come to be thy protector, every day." He then appears before Isis the Great, Divine Mother, Lady of Heaven, Regent of all the Gods, residing in Western Thebes, who bears on her head the hieroglyphs of her name, and he worships her four times ⸢𝍖⸣ in order that she may treat him as Râ, and she replies that "she comes to him"

11

(⟶) 𓏏𓂋𓏏𓂝𓈖𓊪𓏏𓄿 (sic) 𓏤. From the presence of Isis he goes into that of her son Harsiesi, he of the human body and the falcon's head wearing the pskhent, unto whom he presents the wine (⟵) 𓏏𓂋𓊪𓏠, and who, in his turn, presents him 𓏤𓈖𓂋𓂝𓎛𓅆 with the throne of his father Osiris. Again there is a fourfold worship of Hathor, Residing in Thebes (⟵) 𓎛𓊃𓇳𓏤𓏤𓏤𓏤 𓄣𓏏𓈖𓌳𓄤𓊪𓏏𓏏𓏠 in order that she may "put an eternity of joy in his hands," he, Lord of Both Lands, and she accordingly grants that he may rise to Heaven as Râ. On the extreme end of the wall he is seen standing before the mummy of Osiris, Great God, Who resides in Abydos, and he offers him the wine, in order that the god may bestow upon him the gift of life, as Râ, every day.

North-East Wall.—There is but one scene on this small panel: the king standing before Naftâmu, also standing, his lotus-bloom on his head, against a buckle 𓋝 as tall as himself.

At the northern extremity of this chamber, on the two panels which form the right and left of the doorway (Pll. XLI–XLII), stands again the goddess of Truth, Maât; she has the feather 𓏏 upon her head, her arms are swinging, and she waits there to receive the dead king into the Golden Hall, which answers in the tomb to what is in Hades the Hall of Judgment or Seat of Osiris.

THE GOLDEN HALL.

As usual in royal tombs of the XVIIIth and XIXth Dynasties, the Golden Hall is divided in two parts or rooms. The nearest to the entrance is supported by two rows of square pillars, three in each row (Pll. XLI, XLIII, XLVI): two smaller cells open into it, one on the western, one on the eastern side. The second room, in which the sarcophagus stands, is on a lower level; a flight of steps cut between the last pillars of the two rows leads to it, and two smaller cells flank it on each side. The pillars have been left undecorated, and only part of the two rooms has received some decoration. On the south wall, and on the panel of the west wall, which reaches from the entrance door to the door which leads to the first western cell, not only the draughtsman but the painters have been active, and they had made sufficient progress with their work when the death of the king stopped them. The rest of the west wall in both rooms, the south wall, and the part of the east wall in both rooms which extends to the door of the south-east cell, merely bear drawings in black with corrections in red or black : from the door of the cell to the entrance door the east and south walls bear no decoration whatever.   Three of the cells are bare : the western wall in the fourth, which opens into the second room near the head of the sarcophagus, is decorated with an oblong rectangular panel in which the figure of Osiris is painted in vivid colours.

The subjects were taken from one of the mystical books which were commonly used in the tombs of the kings since the middle of the XVIIIth to the end of the XIXth Dynasty, the one which Lefébure called the *Book of Hades*, but which I have named the *Book of Doors*, from the many representations of doors which form its most conspicuous feature.   Lefébure made more than thirty years ago an English translation of it, which was indeed good if we consider the state in which the study of Egyptian religion was at that time : it was published in the first series of the *Records of the Past*,[1] and reprinted quite recently without alteration in the first volume of his *Œuvres Diverses*.[2]   The text in Harmhabi's tomb is very faulty, as any reader can see who will take the trouble of comparing it with Setuî I's or Ramses V's copies.   I have printed it as it is, but I have used for the translation a critical edition which I have made for myself out of the material which is to be found in other tombs, and which I intend to publish later on with grammatical and mythological commentary.

A.—South and South-West Walls.

(*Plates* XLIV–XLV.)

These bear that part of the *Book of Doors* which corresponds to the second division in Lefébure's translation.[3]

A portion only of the scenes in this division has been sketched on these two walls.   At the east end of the south wall the fortified Gateway of the Hours is missing, and missing also its population of snakes and mummies with their inscriptions.   The actual text begins with the picture of the door against which the large snake is leaning : the name of the snake has not been written by the painter, but we know that it was 𓆓𓂝𓈅𓅓 " Guardian of the Mountain."   The regular legend is written alongside its body, but the

---

[1] *The Book of Hades* (*from the Sarcophagus of Seti I*) in *Records of the Past*, Ist Ser., 1878, vol. X, pp. 85–134, and 1881, vol. XII, pp. 3–35.

[2] Lefébure, *Œuvres Diverses*, vol. I, pp. 61–132.

[3] *Œuvres Diverses*, vol. I, pp. 70–73.

lower part of the two vertical columns of which it consists disappeared
long ago :

" He who is on this door he opens to Râ, for says Sau to the Guardian of the
" Mountain : 'Open thy gate to Râ, roll back thy door to Khuîti, for the
" hidden place is in [darkness], that may happen the happenings of this
" God.'   When shuts up this door after this god went in, they that are
" in their mountains wail when they hear the closing of this door."

The upper register was never made, and the place it should have occupied
on the walls has been left blank.   Only parts of the middle and the lower
registers have been executed.

Middle Register.—The boat of Râ, towed by the four ordinary
" people of Hades," meets a company of seven gods, Napina   and
Ninâa with human heads,   Baî "the Soul" with ram's head,   Horus
with falcon's head and the feather   on it,   Ua-â,   Khnumu and
Sazuîti with human heads.   A long inscription runs above them :

" Whereas this great God cruises on the roads of Hades and the Gods of
" Hades tow this God, that he may make the distribution of what there
" is in the earth, to arrange the destinies of those who are in it, to
" weigh the voices in Amentît, to place the great over the little amongst
" the Gods who are in Hades, to bring the Manes to their places and
" the dead to weigh them, to destroy the bodies of the murderers, to
" hale to prison the souls—found empty[1]—says Râ Zaskhuprurîya
" Satpanrîya Harmhabi Maîamânu [to them]: 'Ah give ye to me that
" my crown be restored to me, that I may become possessed of the
" chapel which is in the earth, for Sau and Hakânu have joined me
" that I may act according to your requests and cause to happen your
" happenings.' Saî[2] has restored him his breath, and the offerings which
" are there, he is not shut out from them . . . ."

There stop both texts and scenes at the end of the wall.

Lower Register.—Near the door, and with his back to it, Tâmu stands, leaning on his staff, over four men who lie on their backs, (➤) 𓂋𓂋𓈖𓈖 𓇋𓇋𓅽𓏤 " the fainting ones," and twenty men walk away from those with hands tied behind their backs, six on the south wall and the other fourteen on the east wall, (➤) 𓅱𓏤𓅱𓏤𓏤𓏤 " the defaulters of the great Hall of [Râ] . . . . . " The inscription runs thus, above their heads :

(➤) [hieroglyphic inscription, lines numbered 1–23]

---

[1] The words 𓂋𓏏𓅓 were written in hieratic by the draughtsman or the sculptor to show the master-draughtsman, when he should come to inspect the work, that there was in the original draught of the inscription a blank space which ought to be filled (see p. 62). For other instances of the same case, see further on, p. 81.

[2] The oldest form of the name of Isis found in the Pyramid text as 𓊨𓏏𓇋𓇋𓂝𓏏 *Saît.*

" What Tâmu does to Râ, protecting this god, worshipping [his] soul, causing
 " evils to his foes : ' Whereas true is the voice of my father Râ against
 " you, true is my voice against you ; I am a son issued forth from
 " his father, I am a father issued forth from his son, therefore are ye
 " fettered and your bonds are of stringy strings, for I have ordered that
 " you be tied so as not to open your arms again, and now Râ prevails
 " against you, his soul is armed against you, my father is powerful
 " against you, his soul is strong of will against you, your evils are to
 " you, your plots are against you, your treasons are to you, your
 " retribution is evil ; Râ has judged you and your false testimonies are
 " to you, your evil grumblings are to you, bad is the judgment of my
 " father to you. You . . . . . ' "

The inscription stops there at the extremity of the south wall, although the
procession of chained figures continues on this wall up to the door of the
small room.

B.—WEST WALL : FIRST SECTION.

(Plates XLVI–LI.)

This bears that part of the Book of Doors which answers to the fourth
division in Lefébure's translation.[1]

Beginning at the door of the first cell, we find the vertical line which
serves as a title to the whole scene :

" When this great god reaches this gate, at his entrance in this gate, the
 " gods who are in it hail this great god."

The gate itself is called (←) "the mistress of pro-
visioning." The two mummies with projecting elbows at the entrance and
at the exit of the passage are named, the first : (←)
" Nourita, who stretches out [his arms for] Râ," the second : (←)
" Quaking-Earth, who stretches out his arms for Râ."

_____

[1] Œuvres Diverses, vol. I, pp. 77–82.

The names of the two uræi are: [hieroglyphs] or [hieroglyphs] "She fires up for Râ," and the nine mummies who stand in the passage are [hieroglyphs] "the third Ennead." They say:

(→) [hieroglyphs]

[hieroglyphs]

"Thou hast opened earth and thou hast penetrated Hades, O Sublime One,
"and thou tearest away gloom! O Râ, come thou to us, great God,
". . . . . !"[1]

The Snake [hieroglyphs] "the biter," stands against the leaf of the open door:

(→) [hieroglyphs]

[hieroglyphs]

[hieroglyphs]

[hieroglyphs]

"He who is on this door, he opens to Râ, for says Sau to the Biter: 'Open
"thy gate to Râ, roll back thy door to Khuîti, that he may light up the
"concrete darkness and throw a gleam in the hidden place!' When
"shuts the door after this great god went in, they that are in this
"gateway wail when they hear this door being shut."

The space allotted to this Hour is divided into three registers.

Middle Register.—The boat of Râ, drawn by the four (←) [hieroglyphs]
"people of Hades" in the usual human shape, is seen proceeding towards
a long low chapel, divided into nine rooms, each of which contains a black
human mummy lying on its back: (→) [hieroglyphs]
the "Divine followers of Osiris, who dwell in their funerary chapels."[2]

(→) [hieroglyphs]

[hieroglyphs]

[hieroglyphs]

[1] The word has been left out on purpose by the draughtsman.

[2] [hieroglyphs] *baît* is the Coptic **BH** *M.* **NI**, μνεμεῖα, *sepulchra, monumenta.*

[hieroglyphic inscription, lines numbered 13–47]

" Whereas the gods of Hades tow this great god while he cruises in the crypt
" and acts according to the welfare of those who are in it, [says Râ to
" them] : ' Tow me, people of Hades, look at me, for I am he who made
" you ! Exert your arms with which you are towing me causing me to
" return to the east of heaven, to the places which bear Osiris, that
" mountain mysterious, those lights by which one may wander amongst
" the gods who receive me, when I go forth from amongst you and from
" the crypt ! Tow me, that I may act according to your welfare, unto
" the gate which conceals the people of Hades !' Says Râ to them :
" ' Seeing me, ye gods, attending to me, ye who are in your funerary
" chapels, raise yourselves, for I ordain for you your ways of being ; ye
" who are in your funerary chapels, and watch the souls on the filth
" of whom you live, on the refuse of whom you breathe, rise to my disk,
" expose yourselves to my rays, for your concerns to you in Hades are
" from that which I ordained for you !' Their rations are of meat,
" their beers are of fermented whey, their refreshment is water, and
" they wail when they hear their doors being shut on them."

Behind the chapel, an incline, the first segment of which is painted black
while the second contains water, rises and drops suddenly, leaving a kind

of gulf at the bottom of which the snake ⎯•⎯ [hieroglyphs] lies coiled; on the other side of this gulf another incline, of the same height and length as the first, slowly descends towards the end of the register. On each incline six women are represented standing, the (➡) [hieroglyphs] "Hours who dwell in Hades;" in the horizontal line which runs above the snake, it is said that (➡) [hieroglyphs] "when the snake has given birth "to twelve she flies away and the Hours eat." The meeting between Râ and the Hours is described in the long inscription which is placed above the scene:

"They that stand on their pools, directing Râ on their respective side, says
"Râ to them: 'Hear, Hours, what I decree shall be done for you, that
"you join your gateways, your front part in darkness, your hind part
"in light! Stand up, ye who live on the Snake and what comes from
"it, and whose concerns in Hades are to eat the children of the Snake
"and to destroy that which comes from it; be my guides, for I am he
"that begat you, and I made you that you may do homage to me.
"Join yourselves to you, O my Hours!' Their rations are of bread,
"their beers are of fermented whey, their refreshment is [water, and]
"their rations [are given to them from what comes out amongst the
"Manes]."

Upper Register.—Near the door, and with their backs to it, twelve persons in human shape walk in a line, the (➡) [hieroglyphs] "Gods who pass to their own double." Above them runs an inscription in twenty-two vertical lines:

"They that are passing to their own doubles, who poured libations from a
"fulness of the blood of the wicked mob and of their existence, who
"bring offerings to the place of Râ, says Râ to them : 'Your concerns
"to you, O gods who are in your offerings, are to bring your doubles to
"you and your offerings ; your foes are destroyed, your souls are not in
"the flames of those but [your] souls are in the sealed place.' Say
"they to Râ : 'Honour to thee, Râ-Khuîti ! Hail to thee, Soul who
"stretches on earth ! Hail to thee, Time, lord of years, Eternity
"imperishable !' Their rations are of bread, their refreshment of water ;
"they wail when they hear their doors being shut, and their rations are
"given to them from Him who is being towed towards the gate Precious-
"Souls."

Before those gods in human shape, and walking away from them, twelve
gods with human bodies and jackals' heads are represented, the (⟶) 𓏤𓏤
𓂝𓃀𓃀 "Jackals who dwell in the Pool of Life."
The "Pool of Life" 𓈖𓏏𓏤𓆄 on the bank of which they walk is an oblong
rectangle divided in two parts by a small square cartouche in which its name
𓈖𓏏𓏤 is inscribed. The functions and utterances of those jackals are
expressed in the long inscription which runs above their heads :

[hieroglyphic text with numbers 34–46]

"They that are on the marge of this pool onto which the souls of the dead
"do not rise because of the precious virtue which is in it, says to them
"Râ: 'Your concerns to you, ye gods in this pool, are to watch your
"lives in your pool and to have your offerings from what you watch, ye
"jackals who are laid by your pool.' Say they to Râ: 'Wash thyself,
"O Râ, in thy precious pool, in which the lord of Gods washes, but
"onto which the souls of the dead rise not, for so hast thou ordained
"thyself, Khuîti!' Their rations are of bread, their beers of fermented
"whey, their [refreshment] is wine, and they wail [when they hear
"their doors being shut] on them; their rations are given to them for
"being lords of the sealed place, and dwelling on the marge of this pool."

Close by the "Pool of Life" a second pool is to be found, the (⟶) [hieroglyphs]
"pool of Uræi," on which ten uræi, in two groups of five each, the 
(⟶) [hieroglyphs] "living uræi," raise their bodies and heads:

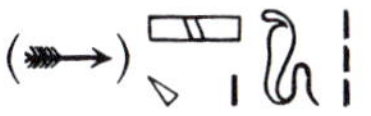

(⟶) [hieroglyphic text with numbers 46–67]

"They that raise their voices after Râ has reached them,—and the souls
"recoil, the shades are destroyed on hearing the voices of the Uræi,—
"says Râ to them: 'Your concerns to you, Uræi in this pool, are to
"keep your heat and your fires for my foes, your fire against those who

12.

" are evil against me. Hail to you, Uræi!' Say they to Râ : 'Come
" to us, O thou who runst over Tanon! Come to us, O thou who
" protectest thyself, for thou art the light of Hades, great god in thy
" crypt!' They wail after Râ has travelled past them."

Lower Register.—Near the door, and with his back turned to it, Horus
(➤) 🦅 stands, leaning on a stick, while eleven gods in human shape, the
(➤) [hieroglyphs] "gods guardians of the diadem," are seen in front
of him walking towards a small naos in which Osiris (◄) [hieroglyphs]
" Khontamentît" is represented standing on a large snake. Between the gods
and the naos the huge uræus [hieroglyphs] " Flame" keeps watch :

[block of hieroglyphic text, lines numbered 1 through 36]

" What Horus did to father Sairi, protecting him and giving back the crown
" to him : 'My heart sails up to my father, my heart is true, my father,
" that I may guard thee against those who act against thee, that I may
" protect thee against those things which threaten thee, for thou hast
" prevailed, Osiris, thou hast ruled, Khontamentît! Thy concerns to
" thee are to reign over Hades, O being of exalted shapes in the crypt!

"The Manes are afraid of thee, the dead are frightened of thee, for I
"have given back the crown [to thee], I, thy son Horus, and I take
"into account thy weakness there.' Say these gods to Khontamentît:
"'Be exalted, dweller in Hades, be pleased, Khontamentît, for thy son
"Horus has given thee back thy crown, he protects thee, he kills thy
"foes, and the power of thy arms is come back to thee, O Sairi
"Khontamentît!' Says Khontamentît: 'Come to me, my son Horus!
"Protect me from those who act against me, and ordain them to the
"Master of Destruction who watches the furnaces!'"

Behind the naos of Osiris twelve gods in human shape are standing, the 
(←) 𓏠𓏠𓏠𓏏𓅃𓃀𓅆𓏠𓏏𓉐 "Gods who are behind the chapel," and Horus
gives them instructions about their duties in regard to Osiris:

(→) [hieroglyphic text with line numbers 36-57]

"Says Horus to these Gods who are behind the chapel: 'Judge for me, ye
"Gods who are behind Khontamentît, and stand up, do not recoil, but
"be strong! Come, partake of the breads of Hu, of the beers of Maât
"and live on what my father lives on. Your concerns in the crypt are
"to be behind the chapel, in accordance with the commands of Râ,
"and I enjoin to you that, verily, you act according to your bequests.'
"Their rations are of bread, their beers are of fermented whey, their
"refreshment is water, and their rations are given to them because they
"are the guardians of the things in the chapel."

Four human shapes, each in front of a vaulted furnace, the (→) 𓇳𓅃
𓋴𓅱𓅆𓏏𓏏𓏏𓏠 "Captains of their furnaces," stand with heads slightly

bowed and with drooping arms : a fifth figure which ought to be at the end of
the register, "the master of destruction," was either forgotten by the artist,
or has been lost :

[hieroglyphic inscription, lines numbered 57–72]

" Says Horus to those gods : ' Ye who have beaten the foes of my father, and
    " who have seized them for your furnaces because of the evil they have
    " done to the Great One who has found the means of my birth,
    " your concerns for you in Hades are to watch your furnaces of coals,
    " according to the commands of Râ, and I enjoin to you, verily, that ye
    " may act according to [your bequests . . .].' "

C.—West Wall : Second Section.

(Plate LII.)

This bears a small part of what is the fifth division of the *Book of Doors*
in Lefébure's translation.[1]

The entrance to the gateway and the oblique passage had been drawn on the
small panel which was between the first and second sections of the wall, but
the limestone was broken and the drawing destroyed : only that portion of
the gateway remains which touched the wall itself, and we can see on it the
last of the hieroglyphic characters which formed the name of the mummy
which stood at the entrance of the passage : (←) [hieroglyphs]
[hieroglyphs] " [The Eater who stretches out his arms] for Râ." Only
the upper half of the wall decorated with [hieroglyph] *khakeru* has been sketched on
the west wall.   It gives the name of the uræus which spits fire (←) [hieroglyphs]
" she fires up for Râ," and in front of it the upper half of the door and of the
snake, (←) [hieroglyphs] " Face of fire," which stands against it.   The upper half
of the two lines of inscription are to be seen on either side of the upper part
of the snake :

[1] *Œuvres Diverses*, vol. I, pp. 82–87.

The lower and middle registers were left empty. The draughtsman placed the figures which were to occupy the upper in what ought to have been the middle : first twelve gods in human shape walking, with slightly curved backs and hanging arms and hands in a posture of adoration, and then seven gods in human shape, walking and holding a rope which winds itself in a kind of coil between each god. The scene ought to have been continued on the north wall, but the draughtsman stopped there and did not finish his work. There is no inscription.

D.—North Wall : Behind the Sarcophagus.

(*Plates* LIII–LV.)

This bore part of what was the sixth division of the *Book of Doors* in Lefébure's translation.[1]

The judgment of the dead is represented on this wall. Osiris is sitting on a platform, with the balance in front of him, at the top of a flight of stairs. Nine gods, "the Ennead which accompanies him," are stationed there each on his stair. Anubis with jackal's head stands in the upper right-hand corner looking towards Osiris, and, under him, a barque is floating in which a large ape is figured beating with a stick a pig, "the devourer of the arm." The legends are in a curious kind of secret writing which exercised the ingenuity of Goodwin,[2] Le Page-Renouf,[3] and Lefébure.[4] The Egyptian artists understood them but little, and were for the most part unable to transcribe them correctly: the man who drew them for Harmhabi's tomb used, moreover, a text which was incomplete, and twice, at least, he was obliged to confess that he "had found empty" places in it where essential words were missing. Lefébure's translation, the best we have at present, is generally unsatisfactory, and the various texts we possess are not sufficiently correct to allow us to rectify the mistakes contained in it. The legend under the throne of Osiris, which describes (⟶) "The two foes of

---

[1] *Œuvres Diverses*, vol. I, pp. 87–91.

[2] Goodwin, *On the Enigmatic Writing on the Coffin of Seti I*, in the *Zeitschrift*, 1873, vol. XI, pp. 138–144.

[3] Le Page Renouf, *The Royal Tombs at Bîbân el-Molûk and Enigmatical Writing*, in the *Zeitschrift*, 1874, vol. XII, pp. 101–105.

[4] Lefébure, *Œuvres Diverses*, vol. I, pp. 87–91

"Osiris" is fairly intelligible, and may be given here as a fair specimen of the kind of text with which we have to deal :

Transcribed into the common script it would be :

" His foes are under his feet, the Gods and the Manes are before him . . . . .
  " he repulses his foes to extinction, and their souls he cuts them
  " to pieces."

The western part of the wall between the scene of judgment and the corner of the room is occupied by three registers of figures—the end of a large text which was not written on the west wall of the room. It belongs to a version of the Book of Hades which is found only in the tombs of Setuî I and Menephtah.

Upper Register.—A mummy, standing on its feet, and held upright by a huge rope at which two men are pulling; three stars are represented above the rope. The men are two of the twelve " bearers of the rope out of " which the Hours go forth " (➡) . Only the last line of the inscription which was over them has been correctly drawn. The rest is a mixture of words written rapidly without reference to the sense they make :

It is easy to recognize in them the end of the inscription which is found in the same position in the tomb of Setuî I :[1]

[1] Champollion, *Monuments de l'Égypte*, vol. I, pp. 773, 774.

The draughtsman had written what he remembered of them as a cue for the scribe, showing him what legend was to be inserted there.

Middle Register.—Two of the " gods who dwell in Hades " [hieroglyphs] walking, and above them an inscription as incorrectly written as that in the higher register :

[hieroglyphic text]

The actual text of line 4 was written on another text, the remains of it are quite legible : [hieroglyphs]. It seems as if the scribe, having forgotten to trace the word [hieroglyph], had inserted it at the top of the line and written underneath his first version. There, also, it is easy to recognize the elements of the formula we read in the tomb of Setuî I :

[hieroglyphic text]

"..... that I may be amongst the mysterious clans who reside in Haît-
" Banbonu (Heliopolis)! Joy to you, and may your souls live, for their
" rations are the rations of Khuîti!" the Sun in the horizon.

Lower Register.—Two mummies standing face to face, and between them a round well full of water, on the brink of which an uræus rises. There is no inscription.

E.—East Wall : Second Section.

(*Plate* LVI.)

The places for the three registers have been reserved on this east wall, but only part of the middle register has been filled with a sketch of the barque of the Sun and the four gods who tow it. There is no inscription.

F.—East Wall : First Section.

(*Plates* LVII–LXI.)

This bears what is the third division of the *Book of Doors* in Lefébure's translation.[1]

The second hour of night is represented on this wall. At one end of it, fronting east, is the vertical line which serves as a title to the whole scene :

---

[1] *Œuvres Diverses,* vol. I, pp. 73–77.

"When this great god reaches this gate, at his entrance into this gate, the
   "gods who are in it hail this great god."

The gate itself is called [hieroglyphs] "Provided with flame."
The narrow passage which leads to it from the region of the first Hour is
watched at its entrance by a standing mummy, whose face is uncovered and
whose elbows project angularly on each side of the body, (⟶) [hieroglyphs]
[hieroglyphs] "Eater of unclean things who stretches out his arms for
Râ," with an allusion to the position of his arms.   After a short horizontal
way, the passage dips suddenly at a right angle, and runs perpendicularly
until it comes to a place where a second mummy stands, named (⟶) [hieroglyphs]
[hieroglyphs] "Groveller in mud (?) who stretches out his
arms for Râ."   The walls of this passage are surmounted with spikes of the
[hieroglyph] kind, and at the point where they turn two uræi rise who spit fire towards
the second watcher and whose name is (⟶) [hieroglyphs] or [hieroglyphs]
"She fires up for Râ," to light him when passing through.   Alongside the
right wall nine mummies of the ordinary type are leaning, (⟶) [hieroglyphs]
the gods of "the second Ennead," and what they say to Râ is written in a
vertical line in front of them :

(⟵) [hieroglyphs]

"The door opens for Khuîti, the gate gapes for the dweller in Heaven ; come
   "thou, this traveller who journeys through Amentît !"

And, in fact, the long and narrow leaf of the door rolls back, against which
the serpent [hieroglyphs], "the winding one," raises himself :

(⟵) [hieroglyphs]

" He who is on this door, he opens to Râ, for says Sau to the Winding One :

" ' Open thy gate to Râ, roll back thy door to Khuîti, that he may light

" up the concrete darkness and throw a gleam in the hidden place.'

" When shuts the door after this great god went in, they that are in

" their gateway wail when they hear this door being shut."

The region in which the dead Sun finds himself is divided into three registers, the middle one of which represents the nocturnal Nile on which his boat floats, while the other two depict the banks between which the nocturnal Nile flows.

Middle Register.—The boat of Râ, drawn by four personages in human shape, the ⭐🦅▱ "People of Hades," is supposed "to be swallowed by the Double Bull," that is to say, to journey inside a kind of long, thin, straight beam with a bull's head at either end, going in at one of the heads and coming out at the other. The whole thing is called (⟶) ⊿ " Barque of Earth," and is borne on the shoulders of eight mummies who stand upright with faces turned in the direction of the Sun's boat, the (⟶) 𓀀𓏤 "bearers." A bull stands at each extremity, near the bull's head, and seven mummies are seated on the beam between the heads of the "bearers." At the farthest end of the beam, the four (⟶) ⭐🦅▱ "People of Hades" reappear, coming out of the bull's head. The explanation of this picture is to be found in the thirty-nine short lines which have been more or less correctly drawn above the figures :

13.

"Whereas the Gods of Hades tow this great god, when this great god has
  "reached the god Barque of Earth, boat of the gods, says Râ to them:
  "'O gods who bear Barque of Earth, carrying the Boat of Hades, your
  "forms raise the light of your barque, precious is what is in it—O Barque
  "of Earth, I have trodden the Boat of Hades which supports my forms,
  "and lo! I travel in the crypt to rule those who are in it. Nurita,
  "Nurita, pleased is the soul of him whom the Double Bull swallowed, for
  "the great god rests in what he created!' Say these gods to Râ:
  "'Whereas Râ is borne high and his soul is provided with the god
  "Earth, his gods are pleased, and the Boat of Hades exults, even this
  "boat!' They wail after Râ travelled past them; their food is of
  "yearly herbs, and they are given their food when they hear the voices
  "of the gods who tow this great god."

Towards the end of the register, the train of Râ meets a party of four human
mummies, standing upright with uncovered faces, and elbows protruding from
the body at a sharp angle, the (➡) 𓀀𓀀𓏏 "swathed ones," and the
gods address them:

"The gods of Hades, in the precious barque which is in Earth, deliver speech
  "to the Swathed whose arms are hidden: 'Your concerns, O Swathed
  "of Earth, who roar for Khentmanitf, ye who have your heads uncovered
  "and your arms hidden, are that breath be to your nostrils, that your
  "cerements be rent, and that your rations be served out to you from
  "what I created.' Their rations are of bread, their beers of fermented

"whey, their refreshment is of water, and their rations are given to
"them from their white mummy-clothes in Hades!"

Upper Register.—Near the door, and with their backs to it, twelve shrines,
rounded at the top, stand in a line with doors open and inside each is a black
mummy, (→) 𓅃𓏏𓏏𓀭𓏤𓊹𓀭𓏤 "the gods who dwell in Hades:" a long
serpent is stretched above them, and above that is an inscription in thirty-
three small vertical lines:

"Those who dwell in their shrines, the divine members on whose shrines the
"Snake watches, says Râ to them: 'Now that your shrines are open,
"and that my light enters your gloom, you whom I found mourning,
"with your shrines shut on you, I give breath to your nostrils, I decree
"that there be plenty for you!' Say they to Râ: 'O Râ, come thou to
"us, great god,' for they perish not they who are before or behind him,
"and his courtiers do him homage, and Râ rejoices coursing Earth, the
"great god travelling in the crypt. Their rations are of bread, their
"beers of fermented whey, their refreshment of water, and the fire
"which is there is given to them that they may live their lives. Their
"doors shut on them after this god passed out, and they wail when
"they hear their doors being shut."

An oblong pool of water, slightly rounded at both ends, extends in front
of them, filling the rest of the register; on its upper marge twelve conical

white shapes rise surmounted with a black human head, and before each of those a huge flag or ear of corn stands.   They represent the (➜) 𓏤𓏤𓏤𓊹 𓁨𓏤𓏤𓈖𓊖𓂋𓂺 "the gods who dwell in the pool of flame," and whom Râ addresses when he comes up to them :

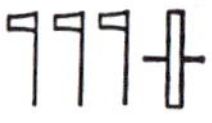

(➜) [hieroglyphic text spanning lines numbered 33–61]

" This pool which is in Hades, it is surrounded with these gods who are
" wrapt up but whose head is bare ; this pool is full of reeds, the water
" of this pool is flame, and the birds pass on when they see its water
" and sniff the smell therein.   Says Râ to them : ' Your concerns as
" gods in the reeds of your pool, ye who have your heads uncovered
" and your bodies mysterious, are that breath be to your nostrils, that
" your food for you be reeds, that your rations for you be out of your
" pool, whose water is mild for you, whilst its fire is not against your
" bodies !'   Say they to Râ : ' Come thou to us, who sailest in thy boat,
" thou whose eyes flame, whose eyeballs sparkle and glow !   The people
" of Hades shout when thou risest, they honour the great god who has
" fire in his eye !'   Their rations are of bread from reeds, their beers
" of reeds, their refreshment is of water, and their rations are given to
" them from what this pool produces."

Lower Register.—Near the door, and with his back to it, ⟨glyph⟩ Tâmu stands leaning on a staff over Apôpi ⟨glyph⟩ the big snake, and nine gods in human shape, the (⟶) ⟨glyphs⟩ "Chiefs who overthrow Apôpi," come towards him.   The inscription above them runs thus:

(⟶) ⟨hieroglyphic inscription, lines 1–26⟩

" What Tâmu did to Râ, protecting the god and overthrowing the fiend:
  " 'O thou that has been knocked over never to rise again, that has been
  " charmed away never to be found again, as true is the voice of my
  " father against thee, so true is my voice against thee, the destroyed by
  " Râ, the tortured by Khuîti!'   They say, the Ennead of Gods of Râ
  " who overthrow Apôpi from Râ: 'Thy head be cut, Apôpi, and cut thy
  " coils that thou mayest no more make inroads in the barque of Râ, no
  " more make onslaught against the divine barque!   May flame issue
  " against thee from the crypt, for we have doomed thee to thy destruc-
  " tion.'   They live from the rations of Râ, from the food of Khontamentît,
  " and offerings are given to them on earth, libations are poured to them
  " as lords of rations under Râ."

A second image of Tâmu (⟵) ⟨glyph⟩ leaning on his staff has its back towards them and its face to a processsion of nine gods in human shape, with ⟨glyph⟩ sceptres and life-crosses ⟨glyph⟩ in their hands, the ⟨glyphs⟩ "lords of welfare," who come towards him:

(⟶) ⟨hieroglyphic inscription, lines 27–33⟩

" Says Tâmu to those gods who have the cross of life and the sceptre : ' Ye
" who are propped on their sceptres and who overthrow the fiend from
" Khuîti, thrust cuts at the Snake Afu the twice-evil worm !' Say
" those gods who charm Apôpi : 'Whereas Earth is open to Râ, and
" Earth is shut on Apôpi, the people of Hades, the princes in Amentît,
" the dwellers in the crypt, they praise Râ, they destroy his foes, they
" protect the Great One against the Snake twice-evil. Ho ! conquered
" by Râ, foe of Râ !' They live on the rations of Râ, on the food
" of Khontamentît, offerings are made to them on earth, fresh water is
" poured to them, as being true of voice in Amentît, precious is what is
" carried in their hidden place. They wail to Râ, they mourn to the
" great god after he has travelled past them, and run away, for darkness
" wraps them up, when their caves shut on them."

Second Western Cell.

(*Plate* LXII–LXIV.)

The second western cell was still undecorated when the king died. Before
the artists left the work, one of them was ordered to paint on the middle
of its west wall a naos, in which Osiris-mummy
was represented standing beside a large *didu* . The surface of the stone
had not then been polished and the colours were laid on its slightly rough
surface, the grain of which partially absorbed it : the picture is not bright,
but the general effect is striking, especially when it is seen in a strong

light pouring in from the Golden Hall through the open door. Two of the wooden figures which were used during the ceremony for the *Opening of the Mouth* were found leaning against the floor under it. We cannot tell exactly what part of the ritual was enacted there, but it was certainly of great interest for the welfare of the dead. From its position in relation to the sarcophagus it might be inferred that it was designed to open a way for the king towards the kingdom of Osiris in the west.

THE SARCOPHAGUS.

(*Plates* LXV–LXXIII.)

The sarcophagus of Harmhabi belongs to the same type as the sarcophagus of King Aîya, the fragments of which are now in the Cairo Museum. It is a large square box in red granite, the sides of which are topped with a high Egyptian cornice. At each end of the long sides a female figure stands with outstretched arms, to which large wings are attached, Isis at the north-east corner facing Neith at the north-west corner, while Nephthys in the south-east faces Selkît at the south-west corner : one arm of each covers with its wing part of the long sides while the other protects the short ones. The lid, which was undecorated, lies on the ground amongst chips of stone. The box itself bears on its sides the usual decoration.

Short East Side (*Plate* LXVIII).—The surface under the cornice presents a square panel slightly sunk into the stone, and surrounded with raised bands, three of which bear hieroglyphic inscriptions. These inscriptions meet in the middle of the upper band thus : , that on the south side ending under the wing of the goddess in the middle of the central panel :

and that on the left ending under the wing of the goddess in a similar position :

14

The upper part of the central panel, under which the wings of the goddesses are spread, contains two inscriptions in vertical lines ; to the right :

and to the left :

Long North Side (*Plates* LXIX–LXXI).—A long horizontal line of hieroglyphs runs under the cornice from the head of Isis to the head of Neith :

On the long panel, starting from the figure of Neith at the western corner, there are to be seen : (1) an inscription with speech by the king :

(2) A figure of Qabhsnêuf with falcon's head and human body half-hidden by the wing of Neith :

(3) A figure of Anubis with jackal's head and human body, to which the following inscription applies :

(4) A figure of Hapi, with ape's head and human body half-hidden by the wing of the goddess Isis :

Short West Side (*Plate* LXXII).—The arrangement is the same as on the short east side, already described, and we find : (1) Two bands of hieroglyphs on the front of the middle of the panel under the cornice, the one on the right side with a short discourse by the goddess Selkît :

the other on the left side, with a corresponding speech by the goddess Neith :

(2) On the central panel, half above, half under the wings of the two goddesses, two inscriptions face each other ; on the right side :

and on the left side :

Long South Side (*Plate* LXXIII).—The legends and figures on it are disposed in exactly the same way as the legends and figures on the other side.

14.

First, a long horizontal line runs under the cornice from the head of Nephthys to the head of Selkît :

(→) [hieroglyphs]

On the long panel, starting from the figure of Selkît on the left side, there are to be seen : (1) an inscription with speech by the king :

(→) [hieroglyphs]

(2) A figure of Duaumautf with jackal's head and human body half-hidden by the wings of Selkît :

(→) [hieroglyphs]

(3) A figure of Anubis, with jackal's head and human body :

(→) [hieroglyphs]

(4) A figure of Amsiti, with human head and body :

(→) [hieroglyphs]

The texts are the same as we find on all coffins and sarcophagi of the time, on those of Iouîya and Touîyou, and Aîya, with a few variations : they are generally finely engraved or painted, but very incorrectly written, and those on Harmhabi's coffin are no exception to the rule. The execution is splendid, and not even on Thoutmôsis I's and Hatshopsouîtou's sarcophagi are the inscriptions and figures better : they look as neat and perfect as if they were all cut in intaglio on some precious stone. Aîya's sarcophagus might perhaps compare with Harmhabi's, but Aîya's has been badly broken, and some of the pieces are missing, while Harmhabi's is intact, excepting a few scratches which were made when the lid was taken away and the mummy desecrated by the robbers.

G. MASPERO.

Cairo, *3rd April,* 1911.

IV.

CATALOGUE OF THE OBJECTS FOUND IN THE TOMB OF THE KING HARMHABI.

By GEORGE DARESSY.

1. **Fragments of the Coffin of Harmhabi.**—Cedar wood. Among the *débris* of wood collected in the tomb of Harmhabi were found pieces of cedar upon which were engraved hieroglyphic signs arranged in vertical columns, 0·08 m wide. Among these fragments, which were all small, was one giving the prenomen of the king. These pieces must have come from a rectangular sarcophagus, or from the sledge on which the mummy of Harmhabi was carried to its tomb. The whole surface had been covered with bitumen.

   Tenons of acacia wood, 0·14 m long and about 0·05 m wide, had perhaps been used to fasten down the lid of the funeral chest. Upon them were lightly incised various religious formulæ: for the protection of the king's body.

2. **Cramp.**—Wood. Length 0·17 m, width 0·045 m. Harmhabi must have had a sarcophagus of siliceous red sandstone (like those of Thoutmôsis II or Hatshopsouîtou) with a split or crack. The joining of the two parts was made secure by a dovetail joint of acacia wood, coated with a yellowish-red varnish of the same tint as the stone. On it are engraved, and painted yellow, lines which form part of the decoration of the sarcophagus.

3. **Canopic Chest of Harmhabi** (Pl. LXXIV).—Alabaster. Instead of making four vases to contain those internal organs of Harmhabi which had to be embalmed, and placing them in a chest, one single object only was made. The canopic jars were cut out of the very same block of alabaster which also served as their covering This had already been done for Amenôthes II. The solidity of the mass no doubt gave hopes of securing the preservation of the remains. Nevertheless, in both

cases the precautions were in vain; the tomb-plunderers had smashed the block into small pieces and scattered the fragments. Only part of these have been recovered.

The chest measured 0·48 m across and 0·65 m high; but it was surmounted by a cornice, made separately, giving it a total height of 0·78 m. The base, 0·19 m high, is ornamented with grooves, both vertical and horizontal, like ▤▤ archaic buildings. The angles are formed by the bodies of the four protecting goddesses of the canopic genii. They lower their winged arms which cross one another and thus cover the entire chest. The same arrangement is also found upon the sarcophagi of Khuniatonu and of King Aîya. The goddesses are sculptured in low relief; the empty space above and below the wings contained inscriptions in vertical columns engraved and filled with green paint.

SIDE I.—BETWEEN SELKIT AND NEPHTHYS.

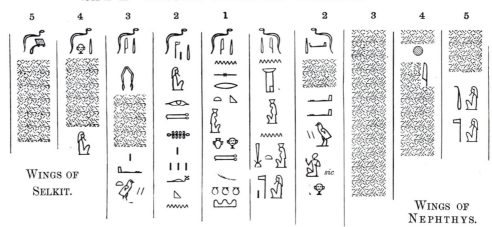

SIDE II.

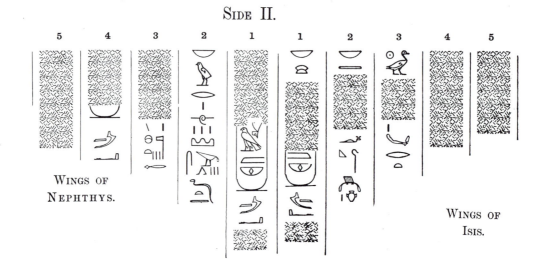

SIDE III.—BETWEEN ISIS AND NEITH.

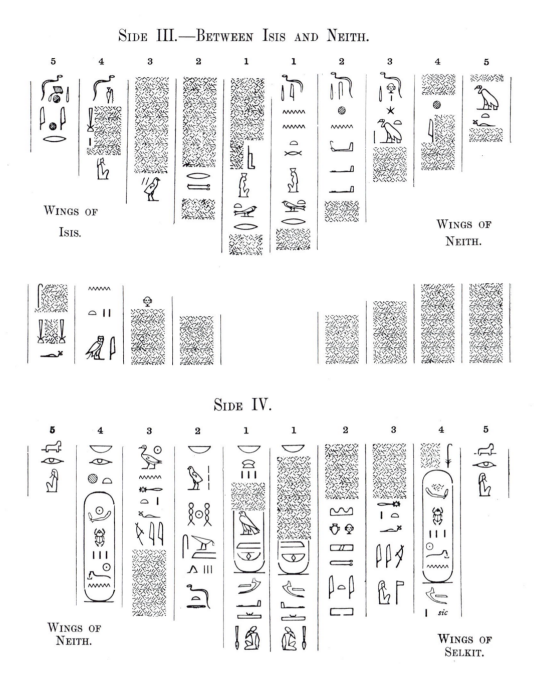

SIDE IV.

Sides I and III give the formula which is ordinarily inscribed upon canopic jars. The changes in the usual order of goddesses and the funerary genii whom they protect are worth noting. Generally—

Isis	is connected with		Amset
Nephthys	,,	,,	Hapi
Neith	,,	,,	Douamoutef
Selkit	,,	,,	Kabhsnêouf

15

whereas here—

Isis	is connected with		Kabhsnêouf
Nephthys	,,	,,	Amset
Neith	,,	,,	Douamoutef
Selkit	,,	,,	Hapi

The top piece had a horizontal inscription under the cornice; only a few insignificant fragments remain: 𓈖𓏏𓀀𓏤𓏤𓏤𓇋𓂋𓁹𓊃𓏤𓈖𓏤 and 𓈖𓏏𓏤𓊖𓏤𓅆.

The cavities intended to hold the embalmed intestines are of the same form as canopic jars. The rims of these pseudo-jars are freed from the mass for 0.05 m in height. Two cross partitions—mean thickness 0.02 m—divide the interior into four compartments and isolate each canopic cavity. Some parts are clean, while other parts are soiled with the bitumen which had been poured upon the portions of the body to preserve them. The diameter of the opening of each of these false canopic jars is about 0.13 m.

Each cavity was closed by a lid of alabaster with a human head, resembling those of ordinary canopic jars. The diameter of the base is from 0.15 m to 0.17 m, the height 0.24 m. These heads are very finely sculptured. The *nemes* or headdress is in stripes alternately flat and grooved; the flat stripes are white, the grooves are filled with green paint. Upon the forehead are two uræi; the beard, the outline of the eyes, and the eyebrows are painted in black; the angle of the cornea is marked with red. These beautiful objects have unfortunately been broken, and there remain only two heads nearly entire (Pll. LXXV–LXXVI).

4. **Canopic Jar** (Pl. LXXVII).—Limestone. Canopic jar, height 0.295 m, maximum diameter 0.17 m. It is of the usual form, uninscribed. The lid, height 0.155 m with a diameter of 0.13 m at the base, is human-headed; the short beard is squared at the end; the outline of the eyes and the eyebrows are painted in black. On the top is written in hieratic the name of a man (?) 𓅱𓇋𓆓𓏤𓅆 *Sanoa*, apparently a foreign form.

5. **Alabaster Altar** (Pl. LXXVIII).—Total length 0.70 m, width 0.31 m, height in front 0.25 m, height at back 0.235 m. Libation-altar of the same type

as the two found by Mariette at Saqqara in a tomb of the IVth Dynasty. In general appearance it resembles certain biers of which the sides are formed of two lions, whose bodies are stretched out and reduced to a rod 4 centimetres wide ; the length of this massive table is 0˙54 m. In front the chests of the standing lions are ornamented by a mane forming a sort of apron ; the locks of hair are indicated on each side of a flat central band, on which is engraved a vertical inscription, the signs being enhanced with blue pigment. On the right : "The Osiris, the king (the beloved "of Amon, Harmhabi), beloved of Anubis in the divine hall, uttering "truth." On the left only the end remains : . . . . ". . . . beloved of Anubis in the embalmment, uttering truth."

The heads of the lions, which were separately sculptured and fixed by a resinous cement, have not been found. At the sides, the front paws are sculptured in detail ; the hind paws are merely outlined in low relief upon the background and are flat, without any carving.

The upper part of the altar is flat, except for a rim of 2 millimetres all round ; the surface is very slightly inclined towards the back, so that the liquids, water, wine, or milk poured upon the table should flow towards the end and, passing through the rim by a groove made in the middle of the small side, are re-united in a conical vase, 15 centimetres in diameter, placed behind the altar, its base being encircled by the tails of the lions.

This altar must have fitted into a socket, as the circumference of the base is not polished for 0˙015 m in height. This most interesting piece was broken into a great number of fragments, many of which have not been found.

The tomb of Harmhabi must have contained several libation-tables like the preceding : at least four. They had been shattered into such small pieces that it is not possible to reconstruct them. The inscriptions, which can be recovered upon the breasts of the lions, read :

6. Statue of Sycamore Wood (Pl. LXXIX).—Height 1˙43 m. Statue of a man, the legs from the knees are missing. It is larger than life ; the

15

height of the remaining part and the dimensions of the head (0·35 m high) show that it must have reached a height of 2·20 m. It was composed of a number of pieces of wood fitted and held together by tenons and pegs. The legs, the left arm, and the face are now missing. It was an image of the king, wearing the *nemes* headdress, clothed in the *shenti* with the triangular projecting apron, 0·65 m wide at the base. The sovereign was represented walking, holding a long staff in the right hand and the sceptre ⌻ in the left. The flesh was painted black; the headdress, necklace, and garment were covered with stucco and gilded.

7. Statue of Sycamore Wood.—Height 1·41 m. The preceding statue had a companion which has reached us in exactly the same state, deprived of the lower part of the legs, the left arm and the face. It was painted black and the costume gilded in the same way.

8. Statue of Horus.—Cedar. Height 0·56 m. Statue of a god walking, the arms hanging, the hands closed. It has the head of a falcon, and must have been Horus or the genius Kabhsnêouf. The whole statue was covered with bitumen, but the necklace was indicated by yellow lines.

9. Statue of a seated God (Pl. LXXX).—Cedar. Height 0·58 m. Statue of good workmanship representing a seated man; the seat, however, is wanting. He is clothed in the *shenti* and wears a large round wig leaving the neck free. The left arm is missing, but it is evident that both arms were held laterally, half raised to the height of the shoulders, and the hands closed. It was probably one of the protecting genii of the tombs, who are represented upon coffins holding a serpent or a lizard in each hand. The statue had been painted black.

10. Statue of Anubis.—Cedar. Height 0·39 m. Statue fixed into a rectangular pedestal, 0·28 m × 0·13 m at the sides, and 0·05 m high. The god, with a human body and a jackal's head, is represented squatting; both hands placed upon the knees holding an emblem which has disappeared, perhaps the whip ⫽\.

The entire surface is covered with a thin layer of bitumen; the necklace is indicated in yellow. Some of the bitumen having fallen off, it is evident that before the statue was blackened there were indications of the eyes, mouth, and costume in black ink.

11. Pedestal of a Statue.—Cedar. Rectangular base 0·235 m × 0·078 m at the sides, and 0·048 m high. It has been used twice, for the two opposite faces are hollowed in grooves which do not correspond. In its final use the holes were arranged to receive the feet of a statue of a man walking, and in front is an inscription in two lines, in yellow :

"The Osiris king (the "beloved of Amon, Harmhabi), beloved of Anubis in the embalmment."

12, 13. Heads of Lions (Pl. LXXXI).—Cedar. Height 0·29 m. Two heads of lions of excellent workmanship, but the layer of bitumen hides the delicacy. The eyes are marked in yellow ; the ear of one is wanting. These heads, 0·49 m and 0·42 m long, must have belonged to entire statues of these animals, but the bodies and limbs have been broken up. Only one tail remains, 0·80 m. long ; it was made of a vine-branch in order to obtain the curve more easily.

14. Statue of a Panther (Pl. LXXXII).—Cedar. Height 0·24 m. Sculptured panther measuring 0·64 m in length to the tip of the tail. The animal is represented walking, the tail hanging down with the end raised. A layer of bitumen impastes the modelling which was very beautiful ; the eyes are painted in yellow. One ear is wanting. Under each paw is a tenon to fix the statue to a stand ; upon the back of the animal are two cavities showing that a statue must have stood upon the panther.

15. Hippopotamus Head (Pl. LXXXIII).—Cedar. Height 0·30 m. Head of a hippopotamus, length 0·60 m, and 0·97 m with the fragment of the back which still adheres, showing that the whole animal must have been represented. The mouth is half open, showing the teeth, which are made of alabaster, and are mostly missing, for there remain only the seven on the right at the back of the upper jaw, carved in one block, with red lines marking the division of the teeth ; the single teeth in front, six below and four above, no longer exist. The ears are mutilated, the fastening only remains. The whole surface was blackened with bitumen.

The hippopotamus was placed in the tomb in order that the deceased king might indulge in the pleasure of the chase, according to an old tradition ; for in the mastabas of the Old Kingdom the deceased is seen in a light boat, piercing with his spear a hippopotamus hidden in the swamps.

16. Hippopotamus Head.—Cedar. Height 0·28 m. Head of another hippopotamus, 0·64 m long, similar to the preceding. The two series of teeth at the back of the upper jaw remain, the rest of the mouth is mutilated. The ears, creased inside like a fan, are here complete. The bitumen has fallen off almost entirely.

17. Jackal (Pl. LXXXIV).—Cedar wood. Height 0·54 m. Statue of a couchant jackal, measuring 0·92 m in length without the tail, which is missing. The eyes, which were inlaid, have been torn out. The whole was covered with bitumen, except the neck which had had a collar of gilded stucco, but the plaster has fallen off, and the drawing of the collar in black ink on the natural wood is visible in its place. The right front paw is missing.

18. Jackal.—Cedar. Length 0·50 m. Body of a couchant jackal, of which the head, the tail, and one hind paw are missing. The bitumen having disappeared almost entirely, it is more possible to judge of the fineness of the sculpture. The claws are made of little tubes of copper.

19. Jackal.—Cedar. Length 0·53 m. Body of a jackal, of which only one front paw remains. Like the preceding, the claws are made of little tubes of copper fitted into the end of the paw. The tail is missing.

20, 21. Heads of Jackals (Pll. LXXXV–LXXXVI).—Cedar. Length 0·09 m and 0·085 m. Two heads of jackals of very fine work ; the eyes and eyebrows were inlaid. The heads may have belonged to the two preceding statues, but could not be fitted as the neck, which perhaps had had a gilded collar, had been shattered.

22. Hathor-cow.—Cedar. In the tomb of Harmhabi there must have been a statue of a cow, almost life-size, which was shattered when the tomb was plundered, and of which only a few fragments have been recovered, notably a foot 0·52 m long (from the ground to the knee 0·35 m). The body of the animal was painted black and was inlaid with numerous little plaques of blue glazed ware, 0·02 m to 0·03 m wide, in the shape of trefoils or quatrefoils, to imitate the spots on the hide, in the same way that the celebrated cow, found by M. Naville at Deir el-Bahrî, is painted. It was an image of the goddess Hathor, mistress of the Theban necropolis.

23, 24. Hawks.—Cedar. Length 0·44 m and 0·43 m. Two statues of mummified hawks or falcons, which must have had some headdress upon the head, probably the solar disk. They are covered with bitumen, the beak and the outline of the eyes are indicated in yellow.

25. Swan (Pl. LXXXVII).—Cedar. Length 0·35 m, height 0·25 m. Statue representing a swan, of which the feet are missing. The neck is curved back and the head lowered, so much so that the beak almost touches the base of the neck. A similar statue was found in the tomb of Amenôthes III; a swan forming a box was found in the pyramid of Dahshur. Nevertheless, representations of this bird, which is no longer found in Egypt, are very rare. It was probably placed in the tomb as a type of the water-fowl which the king might hunt in the other world.

26, 27. Emblems of Khonsou.—Sycamore. Length 0·23 m and 0·21 m, height 0·10 m. Two blocks of wood ⌒ rounded on all sides, having pegs underneath for fixing to stands. This object, a leather bottle or piece of flesh, was an emblem of the god Khonsou, the son of Amon, and frequently figures in the bas-reliefs of the temples carried upon a pole among the sacred ensigns.

28. Germinating Osiris (Pl. LXXXVIII).—Wood. Height 1·525 m, width 0·435 m. Framework for an Osiris of verdure. It is a shallow box (depth only 0·06 m) of which the outline is that of an image of the god standing turned to the right, wearing the *atef*-crown, holding the crook and whip. Small partitions outline the head, the necklace, the arms, etc., and divide the box into a number of compartments; the ground is pierced with holes, more numerous in the head than elsewhere. This figure must have been filled with earth on which wheat or barley was made to grow, in order to obtain an image of Osiris germinating. This process differs slightly from that employed for Maherpra, Iouîya and Toüîyou, for whom earth was simply placed upon a canvas. But it is more like the method used for Amenôthes II where the Osiris is outlined by pieces of wood joined together.

A lid of the same outline as the chest was fastened to it by pegs. It is slightly sculptured *en ronde bosse*, painted in yellow; the details of the body and the ornaments are indicated in relief, and heightened by lines of black and red.

29. Magical Bricks.—Clay. Of the clay bricks which were placed at the four cardinal points of the tomb only two fragments remain. One of them, 0·06 m wide, 0·08 m long, and 0·025 m thick, is surmounted by a rudely-modelled figure of a jackal; this is the Eastern brick. On the other, 0·04 m wide and 0·012 m thick, are several signs of the ritual text which were inscribed in white; it has also a hollow in which the *dad*-emblem had been set; this characterises the Western brick.

30. Troughs in unburnt clay. Eight small clay troughs, 0·165 m long, 0·085 m wide, and 0·03 m high, with an inner hollow of 0·025 m, the edges of which are gently inclined towards the outside. They are probably miniature representations of fields prepared for irrigation, on which were placed grains of cereals, so as to ensure that the deceased should have landed property in the other world, and should harvest the corn necessary for his sustenance. In some of these basins are traces of the water which had been poured over them to emphasise the imitation.

31. Mast of a Boat.—Wood. Height 0·32 m, diameter at base 0·022 m. Upper part of the mast of the model of a boat, which was probably like the galleys found in the tomb of Amenôthes II. It is an exact copy of a real mast showing where the openings were placed, through which passed the ropes for strengthening the mast, supporting the yards, and controlling the sail. At 0·035 m from the top are two lateral appendages 0·035 m long, placed opposite one another, each pierced with two holes, the lower hole being larger than the upper. Immediately below, two narrower wings, jagged at the edge, extend 0·07 m downwards; each has eight holes. Lastly the mast itself is pierced with two holes.

32. Head of a Sceptre.—Wood. Height 0·20 m, width 0·065 m. Upper part of a wand of consecration. It is a blade thin at the edges, thick in the middle, surmounting a lotus-blossom. It was mounted upon a round handle, and the whole must have been covered with gilded stucco. By touching the food and objects with this emblem, and by pronouncing the words of the ritual, the use of the food and objects was supposed to be secured to the deceased.

33. Small Plaque of sculptured wood (Fig. 1).—Acacia. Lower part of a small plaque with sculptures in *relief en creux*. It widens towards the top for a height of 0·038 m, the width at the base is 0·105 m and 0·11 m above; the thickness is 0·004 m. Holes, spaced from 6 to 7 millimetres apart, are pierced close to the edge and show that this object was sewn or nailed. The frame was engraved with a garland of leaves. From what remains of the scene it is impossible to recognise the subject represented. In the centre is a palmetto, on each side stands a man lowering one arm to which a wing is attached. Winged genii are hardly ever seen in Egyptian bas-reliefs; it is therefore probable that this is the imitation of a scene of Asiatic origin, Phœnician or Assyrian. The tablet was probably covered with gold-leaf.

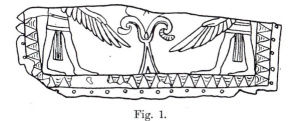

Fig. 1.

34. Leg of a Camp-stool.—Ebony. Length 0·51 m, width 0·045 m, thickness 0·03 m. Leg of a folding chair. Following a design much used for this kind of furniture, the lower extremity represents the head of a goose; the open beak seizes the cross-bar. Behind the eye is engraved a long triangle painted yellow; saw-teeth between four parallel lines, forming a kind of collar, constitute another decoration in yellow. The hole, through which the rivet passed that supported the two legs of the folding stool, is little more than half the length of that piece.

35. Supports of Chairs.—Wood painted white. Two blocks, quadrangular and pyramidal, 0·105 m at the sides of the base, 0·07 m at the upper part, and 0·068 m high, which were joined together by a wooden bar 0·028 m in diameter. It is broken, however, and therefore the original length cannot be known. At the top of each block is a circular hole, 0·05 m in diameter and 0·002 m deep. Four such objects were placed under the feet of chairs. In the palaces of Amenôthes III and Khuniatonu it was found that the floors of certain rooms were made

16

of beaten earth covered with a thin layer of stucco and painted ; and this process must have been common at the time. The feet of chairs would soon have made holes in this coating. To prevent this, large bases specially made to measure were placed under the furniture.

36. Rosettes, in copper (Pl. LXXXIX, 1–5).—Roundels in thin copper, originally gilt, having three or four holes close to the edge for sewing perhaps on harness. They are of two sizes and two types ; the larger are 0·072 m in diameter, the others 0·038 m. Some have a rosette stamped in relief, there are five large and one small of this type ; the others have a five-pointed star, of these there are one large and five small.

37. Pillow, of acacia wood.—Length of base 0·29 m, width 0·09 m ; length of the upper part 0·17 m ; height 0·18 m.

Head-rests of wood or stone, like those still used among the Abyssinians, were employed by the Egyptians to avoid the long operation of curling the hair daily. But a magical idea attached to this piece of furniture, therefore from the time of the Old Kingdom one was placed under the head of the mummy to ensure peaceful repose.

This example is of the ordinary form ; the upright, which supports the concave piece on which the neck is placed, is square with cut sides ; it is not of one block, a piece 0·015 m high is inserted between the upper part and the base ; the whole is joined together by a tenon fastened by pegs, the heads of which are masked by wooden buttons inlaid with ivory.

38. Alabaster Vase (Pl. XC, 1).—Height 0·16 m. Found near the tomb of Setuî I. Ointment vase cut out of a single piece, with a support. The vase, the upper part of which is shattered, is almost spherical, 0·09 m in diameter, surmounted by a cylindrical neck and set upon a short foot, widening to the base. The openwork support has on each of its four faces a transverse bar at half the height, with two diagonal bars above. It is 0·068 m at the sides, and 0·074 m high.

39. Alabaster Vase.—Height 0·09 m ; diameter at the top 0·032 m, at the widest part 0·08 m, at the base 0·054 m. Small pyriform bottle with a flat base, surmounted by a narrow neck and with a small rim round the mouth.

40. Support of a Vase.—Plaited rushes. Height 0·045 m. Support for a light vase, made of rushes. It is composed of a crown, 0·015 m thick and 0·14 m in diameter, fixed upon a square base of the same width, and was used to hold round-bottomed vases.

41. Copper Cup.—Cup in the form of a truncated cone, with flat base. Its height is 0·048 m, the diameter at the top is 0·10 m, at the base 0·04 m.

Besides these objects, there were found in the tomb of Harmhabi remains of objects not worth describing : embalmed intestines wrapped in cloth to imitate the appearance of a small mummy, and which must have been placed in the canopic jars; fragments of statues of men and animals in bitumenised wood; parts of caskets for statuettes or for provisions, in the form of a naos set upon a sledge; covers of provision-boxes in wood, or in the form of ducks in stone; glazed-ware beads from necklaces, cylindrical or thin and wavy like the corolla of a flower; leaves of copper, torn out and bent, etc.

V.

NOTE ON
THE LIFE AND REIGN OF TOUATÂNKHAMANOU.

BY SIR GASTON MASPERO.

Very little is known about the origin of this king. On the lions from Gebel Barkal, which are now in the British Museum,[1] he calls Amenôthes III his father, and the early Egyptologists, Wilkinson, Leemans, Rougé, Mariette, believed him to be a younger son of this Pharaoh, probably by a concubine.[2] This relationship, which, being discarded by Lepsius[3] and Brugsch,[4] had been forgotten for nearly thirty years, was rediscovered by Loret,[5] and accepted by Maspero,[6] but doubted anew by Petrie[7] and Breasted.[8] Taken alone, the title *father*, $\left\langle\!\!\!\begin{array}{c}\frown\\\times\end{array}\right.$, which Pharaohs are wont to give to any of their predecessors, even when these do not belong to their own family, is no proof that there was such close relationship as we supposed, Loret and I, between Amenôthes III and Touatânkhamanou. It is best, therefore, neither to affirm nor to deny that it existed. As a side-light on the matter, we may add that Khuniatonu gave readily his daughters to husbands who were not or were only very slightly connected with his family: Touatânkhamanou may have had no more blood-ties with him than Aîya. Whatever his origin, he came to the throne, under the name of Touatânkhatonou[9], through such a

[1] Prisse d'Avennes, *Monuments de l'Égypte*, Pl. XI; Lepsius, *Denkmäler*, III, 115, 118, 119 *b*.

[2] Wilkinson, *Extracts from several Hieroglyphic Subjects*, p. 11; Leemans, *Lettre à M. François Salvolini*, pp. 68 *sqq.*; E. de Rougé, *Lettre à M. Alfred Maury*, in *Revue Archéologique*, 1847, pp. 120–123; Mariette, *Renseignements sur les soixantè-quatre Apis*, in *Bulletin Archéologique de l'Athénœum Français*, 1855, pp. 53, 58.

[3] Lepsius, *Königsbuch*, Pl. XXX, No. 406.

[4] Brugsch, *Histoire d'Egypte*, pp. 122, 123.

[5] V. Loret, *Tout-ankh-amen, fils d'Aménophis III*, in *Recueil de Travaux*, vol. XI, p. 212; *cf.* E. Lefébure, *Sur différents mots et noms égyptiens*, in *Proceedings of the Society of Biblical Archœology*, 1890–91, vol. XIII, p. 478.

[6] Maspero, *The Struggle of the Nations*, p. 334.

[7] Flinders Petrie, *A History of Egypt*, vol. II, p. 237.

[8] Breasted-Ranke, *Geschichte Ægyptens*, p. 317.

[9] Stele No. 14197 in the Berlin Museum; *cf.* Erman, *Ausführliches Verzeichniss*, 1899, p. 128.

marriage. The daughter he married, Ankhousnepatonou [hieroglyphs],[1]
was the third in the order of birth, but we have actually no means of deciding
whether the event took place during the lifetime of her father or her
brother-in-law [hieroglyphs] Sâkerîya,[2] or whether, having usurped the power
after the death or deposition of Sâkerîya, he legitimated his usurpation by
this alliance. Once seated on the throne, they returned readily to the creed of
Amon : she changed her name to Ankhousnamanou [hieroglyphs][3]
and he became Touatânkhamanou again. His royal protocol, which is nearly
complete, reads thus : [hieroglyphs]
[hieroglyphs],[4] with a few purely
graphic variants of no importance.

The length of his reign is unknown. The signs which expressed the years
on the great stele at Karnak are lost, and his only date is to be found on
Davis's piece of linen : [hieroglyphs] "The good
"God Lord of Both Lands, Namkhouprourîya, beloved of Minou : linen of
"the year VI."[5] It results from this that he reigned at least six years :
whether he reigned much longer is a matter for doubt. Though we have some
reasons to believe that he became a convert to the faith of Amon soon after
his accession, he carried on for a certain time the works in the temple of
Atonou at Thebes : at any rate stones from that temple, bearing his name
and fragments of battle-scenes, are amongst the blocks re-used by Harmhabi
while building his pylons ;[6] some have been noticed in the ruins of the
Maout temple and even at Louxor.[7] Petrie, judging from the number of
small objects which he found at El-Amarna, thinks that he resided at
Khouîtatonou for six years,[8] but no palace and no great tomb of his were

---

[1] Lepsius, *Königsbuch*, Pl. XXIX, No. 392, and Pl. XXX, No. 407.

[2] Flinders Petrie reads the name [hieroglyphs] Samankhourîya (*Tell el-Amarna*, p. 42-43, and *A History of Egypt*, vol. II, p. 234.

[3] Lepsius, *Königsbuch*, Pl. XXX, No 407.

[4] Legrain, *Annales du Service*, vol. VI, p. 192, and *Recueil de Travaux*, vol. XXIX, p. 169; Budge, *The Book of Kings*, vol. I, pp. 150, 151.

[5] See p. 134, fig. 15, of the present volume. The transcription of this small text has been published by Maspero, *Varia*, in the *Recueil de Travaux*, vol. XXXII, p. 88.

[6] Nestor Lhôte, *Lettres écrites d'Egypte*, pp. 94–97 ; Prisse d'Avennes, *Monuments Égyptiens*, Pl. XI, 1; Lepsius, *Denkmäler*, III, 119 a-b; and Piehl, *Lettre à M. Erman sur une découverte concernant le second pylone de Karnak*, in *Zeitschrift*, 1883, p. 41.

[7] Maspero, *The Struggle of the Nations*, p. 335, note 2.

[8] Flinders Petrie, *Tell el-Amarna*, p. 44.

built there in his time, from which we may safely conclude that, if ever he visited the capital of his predecessors, he never stayed long in it. The ruin of the town was retarded, not by the presence of the Pharaoh, but by the activity of the enamel and coloured glass manufactories which Khuniatonu had established in it : they struggled on and kept the district alive for a few years, until the workmen went away to Thebes or to the neighbouring city of Hermopolis.[1] Touatânkhamanou had his customary residence at Thebes or Memphis, probably at Thebes oftener than at Memphis.

He was very active in restoring the supremacy of Amon and repairing the damages that Khuniatonu had inflicted on the temples of this god and of the other Egyptian gods who were included in the persecution. The best part of the work he executed was usurped by his second successor Harmhabi, and it is possible that some of the restorations which have been hitherto attributed to that Pharaoh ought to be reported to his own account. Thus, the great colonnade at Louxor, and some parts of the Phtah temple at Karnak, may be actually his work, though we read now on them the cartouches of Harmhabi.[2] There is no possible hesitation for the fine stele which Legrain discovered at Karnak on the 28th of June, 1905 : the cartouche of Harmhabi had been engraved over his own cartouche, but the rest of the protocol had been left untouched.[3] The date exists no more, as I have said already,[4] and the text presents lacunæ which, however, do not exactly prevent us from catching its general meaning. The historical part begins at line 5, with an exposition of the state of Egypt during the years which preceded Touatânkhamanou's elevation :

---

[1] Maspero, *The Struggle of the Nations*, p. 334.

[2] *Cf.* pp. 23, 56, note 2, in the present volume.

[3] The discovery was announced in Legrain, *Le protocole de Toutankhamon*, in *Annales du Service des Antiquités*, 1905, vol. V, p. 192, and published soon after by Legrain, *La Grande Stèle de Toutankhamanou à Karnak*, in *Recueil de Travaux*, 1907, vol. XXIX, pp. 162–173.

[4] *Cf.* p. 112 of the present volume.

"Now, when His Majesty rose as a king, the temples of Gods and Goddesses
"from Aboù-Elephantine [into the marshes of the Delta were] coming
"to bad hours, their shrines ran to destruction, becoming as *koms*
"on which the cartham prospers, their halls were as if they had never
"existed, their keeps were as a road for common feet ! The land was
"as overridden with ills, and the Gods they neglected this land. If
"messengers were sent to Zahi to enlarge the frontiers of Egypt, it
"never happened that they prospered : if *One* (viz., "Pharaoh")
"addressed a God to consult with him, he came not at all ; if *One*
"prayed to a Goddess, likewise she never came at all ; their hearts
"were sick in their bodies so that they destroyed what had been done."

However, the destinies of Egypt took a new turn with the accession of the
new king :

"So when the days had passed over these things, and His Majesty had risen
" on the place of his father, and he reigned over the three regions
" of Horus, Egypt and the desert being under the place of his face, and
" the countries all bowing to his will, lo ! His Majesty was in his
" palace which is in Pou-Akhpirkerîya, like unto Râ in Heaven, and

"His Majesty made rules for this Land every day without cease.   And
"whereas His Majesty took counsel with His heart and investigated
"every beneficent action, and searched for what was useful to his
"father Amon, and made his august image in pure gold, He did over
"and above what had been done before."

Having thus stated the intentions of the king, the redactor proceeds to
tell how he gave them full effect, making an image of Amon in gold,
lapis-lazuli, *mafek*, and all kind of precious stones, larger than the one
Khuniatonu had destroyed.   He also made for Phtah of Memphis a golden
image of the same kind, but neither in the case of Amon nor in the case of
Phtah do I feel able to understand the full meaning of the text.   So much
for the gods of the two great metropoles.   He then

"raised monuments to the 'other' Gods, he made them emblems
"(   ) of pure gold from the tribute of foreign countries,
"he built their halls anew in constructions lasting for all time and
"made for the sake of eternity ; he instituted for them *wakfs* of daily
"offerings for every day, and he provided for their pastry on earth."
Moreover, "he introduced (   ) to them priests and prophets
"selected from the children of the princes in their cities, and from the
"sons of known persons who knew his name," that is to say who
were likely to serve him readily.   "He increased their sacred vases
"(   ) in gold, silver, copper, bronze without
"limits in their number.   He filled their barracks with slaves, male and
"female, and with the spoils which His Majesty had taken [from all
"foreign countries.   He multiplied] all the property of the temples by
"two, by three, by four, silver, gold, lapis-lazuli, malachite, precious
"stones of every kind, royal linen, white linen, byssus, gum, fat (oil),
"incense, myrrh, perfumes, no end of all precious things.   His Majesty
"built their barks for the river, in fresh acacia wood from the terraces
"of the Red Sea and from the best of the Land of Northern Syria,
"covered with gold from the best of the foreign countries, so that they
"light up the Nile."

Khuniatonu had surrounded himself at El-Amarna with slaves, male and
female singers, tumbling girls (   ), who performed their
office for him or his God.   Touatânkhamanou transferred their allegiance to
the Gods of Egypt, but, as they had been disqualified for it by the service

17

of Atonou, he purified (⟨hieroglyphs⟩) them, before giving them to their new masters.   The phrases which follow are common enough, but, for once, they express the real feelings of the Egyptians at that time :

"The Gods and Goddesses who are in this country, their hearts are joyful all.
    "The shrines exulted, shouted, struck their chests and danced for
    "gladness, after [they had received those things] excellent.   The
    "Divine Enneads which are in the temples, their arms were raised in
    "adoration, they had their hands full of feasts for ever and ever, with
    "life and power all for the nose of" the king.

There is no doubt that the great mass of the Egyptian population must have experienced strong joy when the persecution ended, and the old order of religion was reinstated.   A duplicate of our inscription existed in the temple of Montou at Thebes, a fragment of which is in the Cairo Museum,[1] and copies of it were probably sent to all the great temples to commemorate the event.   No local records came to us of what Touatânkhamanou did in the provinces.   An Apis bull died at Memphis and was buried under him. Mariette discovered the tomb sixty years ago, and he found in it, with pieces of the wooden coffin and a few amulets, the four canopic jars which are now in the Louvre : the king declares himself ⟨hieroglyphs⟩ "beloved of Hapi," as was only natural in the Serapeum,[2] but there is no proof that he was present when the burial took place.   Legrain supposes that the ⟨hieroglyphs⟩ P-âkhpirkarîya, "House of Thoutmôsis I," where he was living at the time he issued the Karnak decree, is perhaps identical with a palace of the same name which was at Memphis and is mentioned on a stele of Aîya[3] ; the restoration of Amon and his cult would then have been planned and executed in Memphis.[4]   But the pre-eminence which is attributed to Amon proves that Touatânkhamanou was then residing in Thebes : if he had been staying in the city of Phtah, he would have spoken more at length of what he had done for its god.   Our P-âkhpirkarîya was in Thebes, possibly a foundation of Thoutmôsis I, where the Pharaohs still held their court occasionally.   Touatânkhamanou was the more likely to take his abode in a palace of one of his early predecessors, that when Khuniatonu left for

---

[1] Legrain, *Un duplicata de la grand stéle de Toutânkhamanou à Karnak*, in *Annales du Service*, 1907, t. VIII, pp. 256–258.

[2] Mariette, *Œuvres Diverses*, t. I, pp. 150–151.

[3] Daressy, *Notes et Remarques*, in *Recueil de Travaux*, t. XVI, p. 123.

[4] Legrain, *La Grande Stèle de Toutânkhamanou à Karnak*, in *Recueil*, t. XXIX, p. 170, note 20.

El-Amarna he must have brought away with him the people who used to live in the palaces of his father Amenôthes III.

A tomb in Gournet-Mourrai has preserved us the only definite record we have of his relations with Ethiopia and Asia.[1] It belonged to a certain Houîya who, having served zealously Touatânkhamanou's predecessors, was promoted by him to the high office of Royal Son of Kashi. Two series of scenes, sculptured and painted on the walls of his funerary chapel, show (1) how he received the vice-royalty, and (2) how he brought to his lord the tributes of the Southern and Northern peoples. When the day came for the official investiture, Houîya was introduced in the presence room, where he found Touatânkhamanou seated on his throne under the canopy. A troop of courtiers followed him with bent heads, hailing the king as they came on :

"Thou art the son of Amon, Nabkhouprourîya, therefore he gives that the
    "chiefs of all foreign countries come to thee, with all the choiced good
    "things of their lands !"

The overseer of the double White House, a roll of papyrus in his left hand, which was a copy of the nomination decree, welcomed him :

"These (the roll of papyrus) are the bulle from Pharaoh, which invests thee
    "from El-Kab to Thebes of Nubia."[2]

Then he says to Houîya :

"Take the seal of office, Royal Son of Kashi,"

and the whole scene is styled :

"The investiture of office to the Royal Son of Kashi, Houîya, from El-Kab
    "to Kali" (the district where Napata lies).

This done, Houîya leaves the palace :

[1] It was described and partially published, first of all, by Champollion, *Monuments* (text), t. I, pp. 477–480; then by Lepsius, *Denkmäler*, III, Pll. 115–118, and text, III, pp. 301–306; by H. Brugsch, *Thesaurus*, t. V, pp. 1133–1141, from copies made by Erman; and by Piehl, *Inscriptions*, t. II, Pll. 144–145. A good English translation in Breasted, *Ancient Records of Egypt*, t. II, pp. 420–427.

[2] *Nastaouî*, the name of the temple of Amon at Karnak, which had been transferred to the shrine of the god in Napata (Brugsch, *Thesaurus*, t. V, p. 1139).

"Coming out with favour from the king, having been proclaimed before the
    "Good God, Royal Son, administrator of the Southern countries,
    "Houîya, that he may account for Khonthannafar and [perhaps "Kali"]
    "which are bound under his will and that he may present them to the
    "Lord of Both Lands, like unto every vassal of His Majesty."

His family and the heads of his own administration adore him, manifesting
their pleasure at his elevation ( ) with common expressions
of praise and wishes: "O Royal Son of the Prince, may Amon in joy receive
"him!—thou shalt enjoy thy happy old age!" According to custom, he
goes immediately to the temple of Amon to thank the god and ask his help:
"coming forth after having poured his praises to him," he goes home with
his wife and sisters and mother and children, with the Sub-Governor of Kashi
, with the Chief of the town Khâmmaît founded by Amenô-
thes III at Soleb, , with the Superintendent of cattle, with
the Sub-Governor of the Station named *Nabkhouprourîya has calmed the gods*
 Pannouît, with the Chief Houîya,
the first prophet , with the priest of Nabkhouprourîya
in the same town, who are bringing him presents. It is rather improbable
that Touatânkhamanou had founded the station which bears his surname: it
must have been one of Khuniatonu's towns in those parts, the name of which
had been changed "to calm the gods" and reconcile them with
the restorer of their cult.[1]

We must suppose that some months, if not years, are past, and that
Houîya is come back to Egypt to offer to the king the tributes he gathered in
the Land of Kashi.[2] Touatânkhamanou is sitting under his canopy as in the
previous scene, and Houîya offers him the produce of Ethiopia, gold in rings
and dust, gold and silver vases of magnificent workmanship, heaps of lapis-
lazuli, red jaspis , malachite, shields, chairs and beds in precious
wood, a chariot. This is:

[1] Brugsch, *Thesaurus Inscriptionum*, t. V, pp. 1133–1141.
[2] Lepsius, *Denkmäler*, III, Pll. 116–118, text, t. III, pp. 302–305.

"The coming in peace, from the house of the Hereditary Prince, priest
    "*Maînouti*, Royal Son of Kashi, Houîya, to receive the favour of the
    "Lord of the Two Lands, to whose neck and arms he has put gold
    "time after time very often.   How great is thy favour Nabkhouprou-
    "rîya !   It is celebrated by word once on the name of Houîya, for it is
    "too frequent to do it in writing !"

Three lines of negroes ranged on three registers come towards the Viceroy.
Those on the upper register are ⟨hieroglyphs⟩ "the chief of Maiâm, O good
prince !"   then ⟨hieroglyphs⟩ "the chiefs of Ouaouaît," and ⟨hieroglyphs⟩
⟨hieroglyphs⟩ "the children of the chiefs of all countries."   Maiâm is the district
between Derr and Ibsamboul, and Ouaouaît the Lower Nubia north of Seboua.
A woman comes amongst the men on a chariot drawn by oxen.   The rest
of the negroes on the two other registers represent "the chiefs of Kashi, who
"say, 'Hail to thee, King of Egypt, Sun of the nine desert tribes !   Give us
"the breath of thy giving, for man lives by thy love,'" and "the chiefs
"of Kashi, who say : 'Very strong ⟨hieroglyphs⟩ are the spirits of our Lord.
"O good God, great is thy power, give us the breath of thy giving, for, O our
"Lord, thou art triumphant'" ⟨hieroglyphs⟩ (lit. "thy voice is true").
In a fourth and last register a stream of Egyptians come out of the house
of the Royal Son of Kashi, Amanhatpou, to greet Houîya and his train :

"When he received the favour of the Lord of the Two Countries."   They said :
    "O prince, excellent, strong in creation, for whom Râ rises ⟨hieroglyphs⟩
    "⟨hieroglyphs⟩), and many are the things of his giving."

At the end of the scene there is a representation of the six Nile boats which
have brought to Thebes the whole train of negro chiefs, prisoners, and tribute :

[hieroglyphic text]

"The coming from Kashi with all this good tribute of the best choice from
  "the countries of the South, and the landing at Thebes by the Royal
  "Son of Kashi, Houîya."

The scenes on which the presentation of the Northern tribute is depicted
are not so fully developed.[1]   There also King Touatânkhamanou is figured
sitting under a canopy, while Houîya is fanning him and holding forth to him :

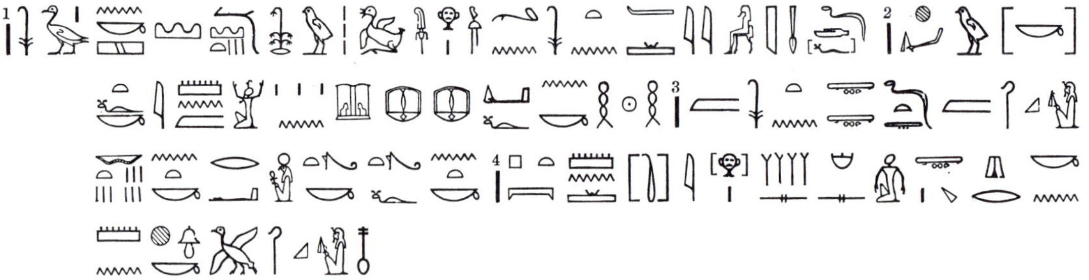

[hieroglyphic text]

"The Royal Son of Kashi, governor of the countries of the South, fan-bearer
  "at the right of the King, Houîya, he says : 'Thy father Amon protects
  "thee through millions of jubilees ; he gives thee time as King of the
  "Two Lands, eternity as Prince of the Nine tribes of the Libyan desert.
  "For thou art Râ and thy emanation is his emanation ; thou art
  "heaven firm [on] its four pillars, and earth sits immovable under
  "thee because of thy beneficence, O excellent prince !'"

Next to him, his brother Amanhatpou, royal Messenger to all foreign
countries, royal son of Kashi, governor of the Southern countries, is represented bringing in all the tributes to the Lord of the Two Lands, the offerings
of Rotanou the vile :

[hieroglyphic text]

precious vases, golden jewellery, heaps of red jaspis and lapis-lazuli, Asiatic
chiefs on two registers.   They belong to the different nations which lived
then in Syria, as recognizable by their different costumes, and they lead a
horse, a tame lion, or carry precious stones, gold, wood, vases finely wrought.
They are divided into several groups, one of which is called Rotanou :

[1] Lepsius, *Denkmäler*, III, Pll. 115–116 a, and text, p. 304.

"The great chiefs of Upper Rotanou, who knew not Egypt since the time of the
   "God, imploring their peace from His Majesty, they say : 'Give us the
   "breath of thy giving, [our] Lord ! Tell us thy prowesses that there
   "may be no revolts in thy time, but that the whole earth be in peace!'"

Others are said to be :

"The great chiefs of the Northern Countries who [knew] not Egypt since the
   "time of the God, imploring their peace from His Majesty."

The rest represented "all the great chiefs of the
far-away countries" who came to render homage to the king, for "there is no
one may live who ignores thee!" Such are the principal features of the scenes:
those at least which may help us to recover part of Touatânkhamanou's
history.

They give us the impression that the whole of Ethiopia was still in his
power: the presence of a group of prisoners in chains is easily explained,
when we remember that, even under the most prosperous kings of the
XVIIIth Dynasty, the desert tribes were for ever encroaching on the Egyptian
territory, and that, as a natural consequence, the Egyptian officers were
obliged to send *rezzous* against them to restore tranquillity on the borders.
With that exception, all the Ethiopians who appeared in the train were
vassal chiefs or sons of chiefs who came to renew their allegiance to the
king ; we may even presume that the princess was the daughter or sister
of one of them and that she was being brought to Egypt as a hostage in the
harem of Pharaoh. But while nobody contests the reality of the Ethiopian
scenes in Houîya's tomb, doubts have been raised against the sincerity of the
Syrian. First of all, they are not so fully developed as the Ethiopian, and
we do not observe in them the same variety of tributary nations that are to
be found in the tombs of Manakhpiriya-sanbi, for instance, or Amounazhe.[1]
Moreover, they are led by two *Royal Sons of Kashi*, Houîya and his brother
Amanhatpe, and "this looks suspicious. What should the viceroy of Koush

[1] Max Müller, *Egyptological Researches*, t. II, pp. 1–49, and Pll. 1–35.

"have to do with the tribute of the North? Moreover, we know from the
"Amarna Letters that Egyptian power in Asia was at an end under Ikhnaton.
"One might be inclined to think, therefore, that the frequent representation
"of the tribute of the South and North in earlier Theban tombs of the
"XVIIIth Dynasty induced Huy to add the tribute of the North as a pendant
"to the tribute of the South which he actually collected." Breasted, however,
ends by admitting that there may have been an element of reality in the
Syrian series of pictures. "It should not be forgotten that one of Ikhnaton's
"successors carried on war in Asia,[1] and this can hardly be any other than
"Tutankhamon. He may thus have been able to collect some northern
"tribute." [2]

I think that Breasted is right, and that the objections are not as decisive
as some have said they were. I am not prepared to allow that "we know
"from the Amarna Letters that Egyptian power was at an end under
"Ikhnaton" or Khuniatonu. We possess a small part only of the correspondence which was exchanged during those years between the court of
Egypt and its vassals in Asia; it is, to say the least, imprudent to declare
that, because we have no more letters, there were no more of them showing
that Khuniatonu retained part of the territories he had inherited there from
his father. It is true that, as far as we can gather from a study of the
existing correspondence, trouble and war raged everywhere in the Syrian
provinces : the land on the Euphrates and Orontes was lost and with it part
of Northern Phœnicia, but that is no reason why the south of Phœnicia and
the whole of Canaan should not be still under the sovereignty of Egypt.
An inscription in the tomb of another Houîya at El-Amarna records that, in
the twelfth year of his reign, Khuniatonu received the tributes of Khairou
with those of Kashi,[3] and it is quite possible, if not probable, that after his
death such tributes were brought over to Egypt from time to time. The
people of Canaan were harassed on the northern borders by the Khatis, and
on the southern and eastern by the Khabiri ; not being strong enough to
resist their attacks, it was but natural that they should claim help from the
power who had conquered and governed them for nearly two centuries.
Even if there were not a few Egyptian outposts left in strategical points of
importance, there was always a chance that Pharaoh might send a small

---

[1] *Cf.* p. 15 *sqq.* of the present volume, where I have tried to show that those Syrian wars
were carried on by Khuniatonu himself.

[2] Breasted, *Ancient Records of Egypt*, t. II, pp. 422–423.

[3] Lepsius, *Denkmäler*, III, Pl. 100 *b*; M. de G. Davies, *The Rock Tombs of El-Amarna*
pp. 9–12, and Pll. XIII–XV.

body of troops to their relief in case they approached him with presents in a propitious hour. When we remember how perseveringly the small Hebrew and Palestinian princes turned to the Ethiopian and Saitic kings for protection against the Assyrian and Babylonian invaders seven or eight centuries later, at a time when Egypt was no more the all-powerful State it had been, we need not wonder if the chiefs of Kharou, Zahi or Rotanou, who had seen the glorious days of Amenôthes III, were ready to put their trust even on his weak successors. The probabilities are that the scenes in Houîya's tomb record an actual incident of this kind. Houîya happened to be in Thebes when the Asiatics came to implore assistance, and, as he was evidently a favourite with Pharaoh, he was entrusted with the care of introducing them to the presence : it was not unusual for men of high standing, whatever their ordinary functions, to introduce thus foreign embassies, and Rakhmirîya, his son Manakhpirîya-sanabi, Amounazhe under Thoutmôsis III had acted in the same way both for Koushite and for Asiatic or European tribute-bearers. Only one point is obscure in the present case, the coexistence of two viceroys of Ethiopia, Houîya and his brother Amenôthes. I am ready to admit that Amenôthes succeeded his brother Houîya in the dignity, and that he took part in the pageant before departing for his province ; but it is no more than a supposition.

Such are the few facts we know about Touatânkhamanou's life and reign. If he had children by his queen Ankhousnamanou or by another wife, they have left no trace of their existence on the monuments : when he died, Aîya replaced him on the throne, and buried him. I suppose that his tomb was in the Western Valley, somewhere between or near Amenôthes III and Aîya : when the reaction against Atonou and his followers was complete, his mummy and its furniture were taken to a hiding-place, as those of Tîyi and Khuniatonu had been, probably under Harmhabi, and there Davis found what remained of it after so many transfers and plunders. But this also is a mere hypothesis, the truth of which we have no means of proving or disproving as yet.

CAIRO, 1st June, 1912.

VI.

CATALOGUE OF THE OBJECTS FOUND IN AN UNKNOWN TOMB, SUPPOSED TO BE TOUATÂNKHAMANOU'S.

---

1. Funerary Statuette (Pl. XCI).—Alabaster. Height 0·235 m. Magnificent funerary statuette in fine translucent alabaster. The deceased is represented in civilian costume of state, the arms crossed upon the breast. The hair is carefully arranged in tiers of little locks beside the face, while above and at the back it hangs regularly, starting from the top of the head. The costume comprises a wide plaited robe, with large sleeves ending above the elbow, forming in front an apron stiffened and projecting. Round the loins is knotted a broad scarf, the fringed end hanging over the upper part of the apron. This method of wearing a scarf, quite different from the Egyptian *shenti*, appears to be an Asiatic importation, for this piece of apparel forms part of the traditional costume of the Syrians, whereas it is not represented in Egypt before the reign of Amenôthes III. It appears to have been a distinctive badge of personages of high rank, notably fan-bearers and officers of the royal household. Unfortunately there is no inscription to give us the name of the dignitary thus represented, who may have been Aîya before his elevation to the throne.

Fragments of gold-leaf, torn into small pieces, crushed or made into pellets, were collected in the tomb. Some pieces, very thin and flat, must have been stripped by the plunderers from furniture or funerary objects; other pieces, a little thicker, are engraved and must have been nailed or stitched upon toilet implements, harness, quivers, etc. After spreading out the latter, I succeeded in reconstructing some designs, more or less incomplete. Generally, however, it is impossible to recognise from the shape the object which was originally

18.

covered by the gold-leaf. The following are the pieces to point out :—

2. Piece of Gold-leaf (Fig. 2).—Height 0·19 m, width 0·13 m. Plaque wider below than above, rounded at the top and indented at the base. This may have formed the middle of a fan or fly-flap. In the middle is a large *sam* , the emblem of union, occupying the whole height of the plaque. Two captives, an Asiatic and a negro, are bound to it with

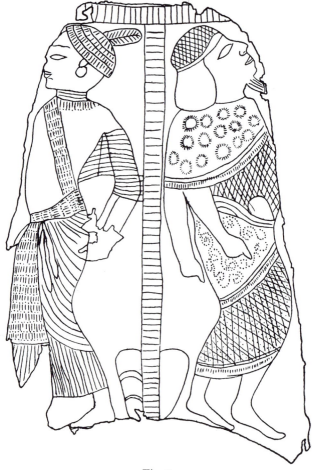

Fig. 2.

their arms behind their backs. The former has a small beard, thick hair forming a bunch on the neck, and a skull-cap with lozenge-shaped stripes covers the head. The robe is checked, and the cape which covers the shoulders is ornamented with suns or circles in divergent lines. A wide scarf encircling the waist is made of some material with trails drawn in dots. He is the type of the Syrian from the North of Palestine, Phœnicia, or Canaan.

The negro's hair is divided into four tiers of plaits, and a feather is stuck on the top of his head. He is clothed in a long robe, the lower part plaited. A long scarf passes over his right shoulder, crosses his chest, and is twisted round his loins like a girdle, the end hanging down in front of his legs.

3. Piece of Gold-leaf (Fig. 3).—Length 0·20 m, height 0·103 m. Elongated plaque, narrower at one end than at the other, which may have ornamented the end of a quiver. King Aîya, whose cartouches are , is represented standing upon his chariot, drawing a bow. The bodies of the two richly-caparisoned horses are covered with a check cloth and their heads are surmounted

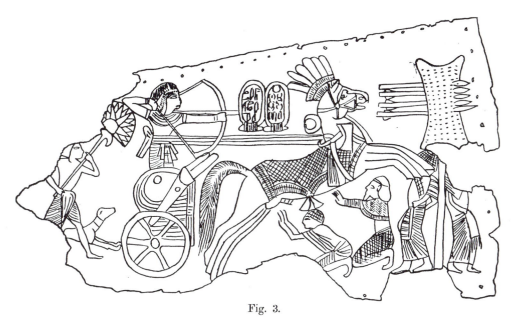

Fig. 3.

by long plumes. They are guided by the king himself, who has fastened the reins to his girdle. His hair is divided into several superposed tiers of little locks, a broad collar covers the upper part of his chest, bracelets are on his arms, and the *shenti* plaited horizontally is ornamented in front with the royal scarf. The chariot is mounted upon wheels with six spokes, and has a quiver attached to the side.

Behind the chariot walks an officer carrying the great *flabellum*, and an animal like a dog with a long muzzle and wearing a collar is seen running. This is the first representation of a greyhound in a scene of this kind ; it is usually a lion that accompanies the Pharaoh in his expeditions.

Under the horses kneel a negro and an Asiatic, raising their arms and petitioning the king. Farther off, a large sign ⟨sign⟩ planted in the earth, a kind of target made of an animal's hide, is pierced with four arrows, and two captives are fastened to the stake. The sign ⟨sign⟩ *sati* means "To draw or shoot arrows." The symbolism of the scene is thus easy to understand. The king, when he goes on a campaign against his enemies, goes to it as to a hunting-party, and the foreigners implore him not to take them as targets for his arrows which never miss their mark.

4. Piece of Gold-leaf (Fig. 4).—Length 0·136 m, height 0·083 m. Gold plating forming a horizontal band with a flat triangular piece below ornamented with a lotus blossom.

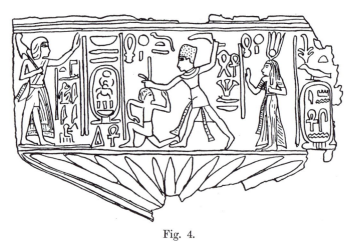

Fig. 4.

The principal scene represents Touatânkhamanou, helmet on head, brandishing the *harpé* with which he is about to strike a kneeling Libyan whom he holds by the hair. The texts which refer to the king are ⟨hieroglyphs⟩ "Lord of the two lands (Nab-khouprou-rîya) giving life for ever like the sun." Behind him stands the "great royal wife (Ankhousnamânou)," dressed in an ample robe, with the headdress of Hathor, two long plumes, the disk and horns. As the substitute of this goddess she makes the gesture of protection, which is explained by ⟨hieroglyphs⟩ "All protection of life is behind him, like the sun."

Facing the king is a person who bears the fan, which is the sign of high officials; he is called ⟨hieroglyphs⟩ "The divine father Aîya."

It is evidently the same man who ascended the throne and was one of the ephemeral kings at the end of the XVIIIth Dynasty. There has been long hesitation in deciding whether Touatânkhamanou or Aîya reigned first. This scene supports the arrangement now generally adopted, it proves that Aîya was only one of the high functionaries in the time of Touatânkhamanou and succeeded the latter.

5. **Piece of Gold-leaf** (Fig. 5).—Length 0·192 m, height 0·113 m. Plaque, of which nearly all the edges are missing. On the left are engraved the two cartouches of King Aîya, placed upon the sign of gold. Three foreigners salute the name of the king. The

Fig. 5.

first has a large beard and thick hair falling on the neck; his garment is ornamented with dotted designs forming circles above and squares below; the cape and broad girdle are also decorated. This is the traditional type of the Syrian from the Mediterranean coasts.

The second has the hair arranged in tiers and surmounted by a feather, the collar fits closely to the neck, the scarf crosses the breast, and the robe falls in straight folds. He is undoubtedly a negro of the Soudan.

The third wears a pointed beard; in his flowing hair are fixed two plumes; a large cloak envelops the body leaving the limbs bare. It is in this way that, in the tombs of the kings and other ethnographical pictures, are represented the Tahennou and Tamahou, viz. : the white-skinned races of the North, Libyans of Marmarica and inhabitants of the Mediterranean islands. Here, then, is a representation of the three Biblical races, Shem, Ham, and Japhet.

Towards the right there appear to have been inscriptions super-imposed and effaced.

6. Piece of Gold-leaf (Fig. 6).—Height 0·09 m, length 0·07 m. Fragment of gold-leaf, belonging to the extreme left side. A king with a helmet on his head draws a bow towards the right ; he wears a broad necklace and bracelets ; for clothing he has only the striped *shenti* with the royal girdle. He is seated upon a camp-stool covered with an animal's (panther's ?) skin, the feet and tail of which hang down.

Behind the king is a quiver laid upon the ground ; next to it is the sign of life ♀ with arms holding a *flabellum*. The inscriptions are destroyed.

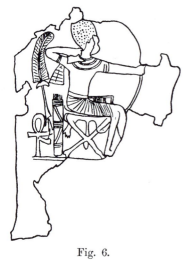

Fig. 6.

7. Piece of Gold-leaf (Fig. 7).—Length 0·09 m, height 0·075 m. Right side of a gold plaque upon which the king was represented under the form of a sphinx or human-headed lion, trampling upon fallen enemies. Only a few signs from the inscriptions remain : [□] □ × [☵] "Treading down the foreigners," and [⚨] ⚱ ⌣ "All protection of life behind him."

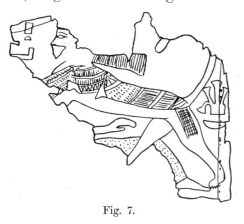

Fig. 7.

8. Piece of Gold-leaf (Fig. 8).—Height 0·062 m, width 0·052 m. Plaque rounded at the bottom. In the upper part three cartouches are placed vertically (⊙🪲⎵), (𓇳 ♀ 🦢), and (𓇳 ♀ 〰). The first two are the names of the king Touatânkhamanou, the last that of his wife, Ankhousnamânou. They surmount the sign, the emblem of the union of the South and the North ; the whole signifies that the entire world is under the authority of the Pharaoh.

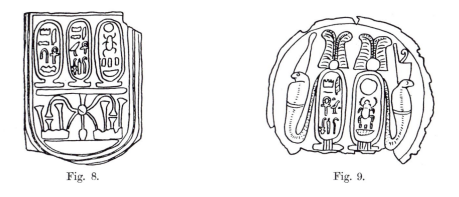

Fig. 8.   Fig. 9.

9. Piece of Gold-leaf (Fig. 9).—Diameter 0·07 m. Circular plaque. The two cartouches of Touatânkhamanou and are arranged vertically, each surmounted by the disk and two feathers. They had been placed upon the signs, which have disappeared with a piece of the plaque. Two great uræi are on each side of them, one wearing the crown of the South, the other the crown of the North.

10. Piece of Gold-leaf (Fig. 10).—Height 0·14 m, width 0·084 m. Two plaques, the tops of which were pointed or rounded. The upper part bears a large inverted lotus ; the central part is decorated with three groups, each one composed of a full-blown lotus between two buds ; and in the middle is a circular opening. Towards the bottom there are three wreaths one above the other ; the first is composed of flowers seen from the front, the second of leaves or buds, the third of alternate flowers and buds of papyrus.

11. Piece of Gold-leaf (Fig. 11).—Height 0·11 m, width 0·085 m. Rectangular plating of gold. In the middle of the lower part, which stands out in relief, is a conventional flower or palmetto, surrounded by three wreaths, which are arranged in a horse-shoe. The first and third row are of leaves alternately plain and pricked ; the middle row represents small flowers seen from the front. In the angles above are lotuses. The upper part is filled with garlands arranged horizontally across the whole width of the plaque ; the first is made of smooth leaves upon a dotted ground, the second of round grains.

There must have been in the tomb a certain number of ornaments of this type, at least four of the same size and two larger, 0·18 m wide.

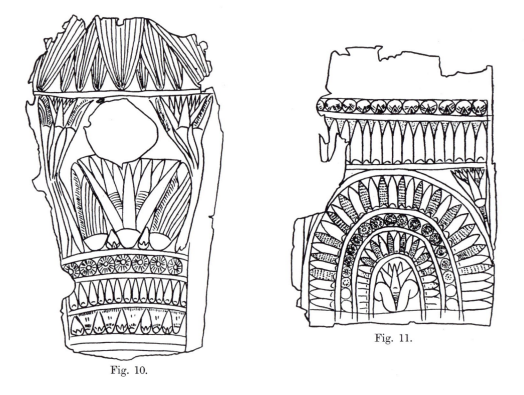

Fig. 10.

Fig. 11.

For the latter the number of wreaths encircling the central palmetto reaches five, but the elements are always the same.

12. **Piece of Gold-leaf** (Fig. 12).—Length 0·202 m, height 0·036 m. Horizontal band ornamented with palmettos of two different designs alternately upon a wavy line which supports them all at the bottom. One of the palmettos has seven leaves, of which the four lower ones have

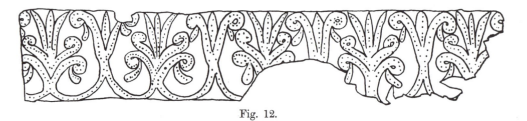

Fig. 12.

their ends twisted in opposite directions to one another. The palmettos of the second type have only three leaves, the two on either side forming volutes. Stalk and flowers are accentuated by being powdered with dots.

13. Piece of Gold-leaf (Fig. 13).—Diameter 0·064 m. Five roundels engraved with the same design. Rosette of four petals between which are lotus blossoms. The execution is careless.

14. Piece of Gold-leaf (Fig. 14).—Width 0·024 m. Several pieces of a long vertical band, engraved with palmettos of two different types, usually alternating. The sketch gives a specimen of these two palmettos, which are very irregularly drawn and much effaced.

Fig. 13.   Fig. 14.

15. Various pieces of Gold-leaf.—There are, besides, other scraps of gold-leaf, either too small to show the subject engraved upon them, or bearing incomplete inscriptions :

1. Upper part of a rounded plaque, 0·088 m long, 0·028 m high. It has the cartouche of the prenomen ⌜⊙ 𓆣 𓆣⌟ of King Aîya, and at the sides two bound negroes.

2. Fragment of the left side of a piece of gold-leaf (height 0·088 m, width 0·055 m) which must have been very large judging by the size of the hieroglyphs (width 0·02 m). These give the end of the name of Aîya 𓏛 𓏤𓏤 𓃒 𓏥 𓏲.

3. Scraps of a piece of gold-leaf upon which were enumerated the titles of Aîya before his elevation to royalty. There remain only : 𓉐 𓂦 𓄿 [𓂺] 𓈒 ; 𓈒 𓂋 𓅬 𓏤 𓈒 ; 𓈒 𓃟 𓂓 𓊋 𓏤 𓈒 𓇳 𓈖 𓇳 𓏏 "Prince and chieftain, royal chancellor . . . fan-"bearer . . . judge acting justly, prophet of Mâît, reuniting the "gods(?)."

4. Two pieces of a plaque of gold, thick and stiff, which also bears the titles of the same functionary, 𓊪 𓂋 𓈒 and 𓅆 𓈗 𓏤 𓁐 𓈒 .

16. Uræi, of gilded bronze.—Eighteen small uræi 𓆗 of gilded bronze, height 0·025 m, furnished at the back with a tang 0·015 m long to fix them perhaps as ornaments on the top of a piece of furniture, or perhaps on the forehead or round the crown of a statue.

17. Knobs from Furniture (Pl. XC, 2–3).—Alabaster. Four knobs from furniture, probably for clothes chests. These studs are of alabaster, the heads slightly convex, hollowed laterally like the groove of a pulley, the base being encircled by a fillet. The diameter varies from 0·06 m to 0·078 m, and the height from 0·055 m to 0·06 m. The axis is hollow and pierced by a bronze nail about 0·20 m long, of which the gilt head, from 0·026 m to 0·028 m in diameter, was visible in the centre of the stud, while the point of the nail after having passed through the thickness of the coffer or lid had been beaten back at a right angle and thus securely fastened the stud to the piece of furniture.

Fig. 15.

18. Knobs from Furniture (Pl. LXXXIX, 6).—Glazed ware. Two buttons for furniture, of blue glaze, in the form of a lenticular disk, 0·068 m in diameter and 0·02 m in thickness, convex above, flat below, and with a square hole for driving in a wooden peg to fasten it to the box.

On the face, one has the prenomen ⟨cartouche⟩, the other the nomen ⟨cartouche⟩, of King Aîya, placed vertically upon the sign of gold, and surmounted by the disk and two plumes 𓂉, and flanked by two uræi, one wearing the crown of the South 𓋹, the other the crown of the North 𓋾.

19. Knob from Furniture (Pl. LXXXIX, 7).—Glazed ware. Knob of furniture in blue-green glaze, more elongated than the preceding, 0·045 m high, with a diameter of 0·018 m at the base and a maximum width of 0·03 m. Round the lower part there are two grooves filled with plaster to fix the inlays of stone or variegated glazes. Underneath is a square hole for fastening the object to a peg.

20. Linen.—Piece of linen (Fig. 15), on which is written an inscription of the sixth year in Touatânkhamanou's reign. It was originally published by Maspero, *Varia*, § 1, in *Recueil de Travaux*, vol. XXXII, p. 88.

21. Blue Glaze Vase, with cartouche of Touatânkhamanou (Pl. XCII).— This vase was not actually found in the Tomb of Touatânkhamanou, but in a hiding-place, under a large rock, some little distance from the tomb.

PLATE I.

CONTINUATION OF THE VALLEY LEADING TO THE GATE.

PLATE II.

THE GATE.

PLATE III.

INSIDE THE GATE SHEWING THE DONKEY STAND.

PLATE IV.

TWO RAMSES TOMBS TO THE RIGHT OF THE ENTRANCE. OPENED IN 1905-1906.

PLATE V.

TOMBS OF RAMSES IX AND QUEEN TÎYI.

PLATE VI.

PATH LEADING TO HARMHABI'S TOMB.

PLATE VII.

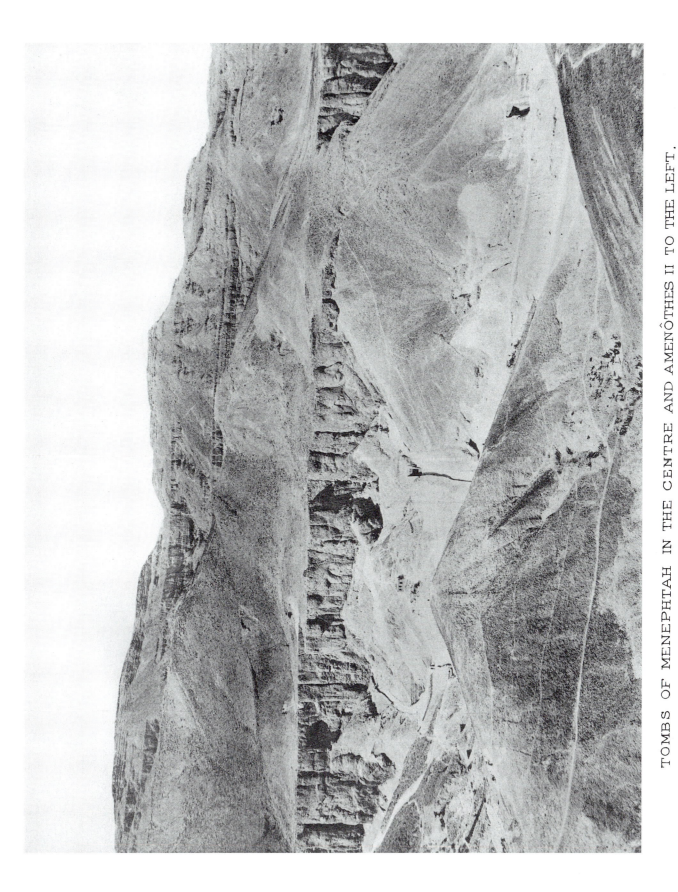

TOMBS OF MENEPHTAH IN THE CENTRE AND AMENÔTHES II TO THE LEFT.

PLATE VIII.

PATH LEADING FROM THE TOMB OF THOUTMÔSIS IV.

PLATE IX.

PATH ON THE EXTREME RIGHT LEADS TO THOUTMÔSIS IV, ON THE EXTREME
LEFT IS THE TOMB OF QUEEN HATSHOPSOUÎTOU, IN THE CENTRE TOMB OF A
PRINCE OF THE XX DYNASTY.

PLATE X.

EXCAVATIONS OF Mr DAVIS. 1909-1910.

PLATE XI.

EXCAVATIONS OF MR DAVIS 1909-1910.

PLATE XII.

EXCAVATIONS OF Mʳ DAVIS 1909-1910.

PLATE XIII.

PLATE XIV.

TOMB OF SIPHTAH ON THE LEFT.

PLATE XV.

STEPS LEADING TO THE TOMB OF THOUTMÔSIS III ON TOP OF
THE MOUNTAIN.

PLATE XVI.

VIEW FROM THE MOUNTAIN LOOKING FROM THE TOMBS OF THE KINGS.

PLATE XVII.

VIEW FROM THE MOUNTAIN LOOKING TOWARDS THE TOMBS OF THE KINGS.

PLATE XVIII.

ROAD LEADING FROM THE TOMBS.

PLATE XIX.

Mʳ DAVIS' HOUSE AT THE ENTRANCE OF THE WESTERN VALLEY.

PLATE XX.

VIEW IN THE WESTERN VALLEY.

PLATE XXI.

VIEW IN THE WESTERN VALLEY.

PLATE XXII.

VIEW IN THE WESTERN VALLEY.

PLATE XXIII.

BEGINNING OF THE FIRST RAMP.

PLATE XXIV.

END OF FIRST INCLINE.

PLATE XXV.

WELL ROOM SOUTH WEST WALL AND SOUTH PART OF WEST WALL.

PLATE XXVI.

WELL ROOM NORTH PART OF WEST WALL AND REMAINS OF NORTH WALL.

PLATE XXXV.

ROOM PRECEDING THE GOLDEN HALL.

SOUTH EAST WALL ABUTTING TO EAST WALL.

PLATE XXXVI.

ROOM PRECEDING THE GOLDEN HALL.

SOUTH PART OF EAST WALL.

PLATE XXXVII.

ROOM PRECEDING THE GOLDEN HALL.

NORTH PART OF EAST WALL.

PLATE XXXVIII.

EAST WALL:
HARMHABI OFFERING WINE TO ANUBIS.

PLATE XLVII.

GOLDEN HALL.

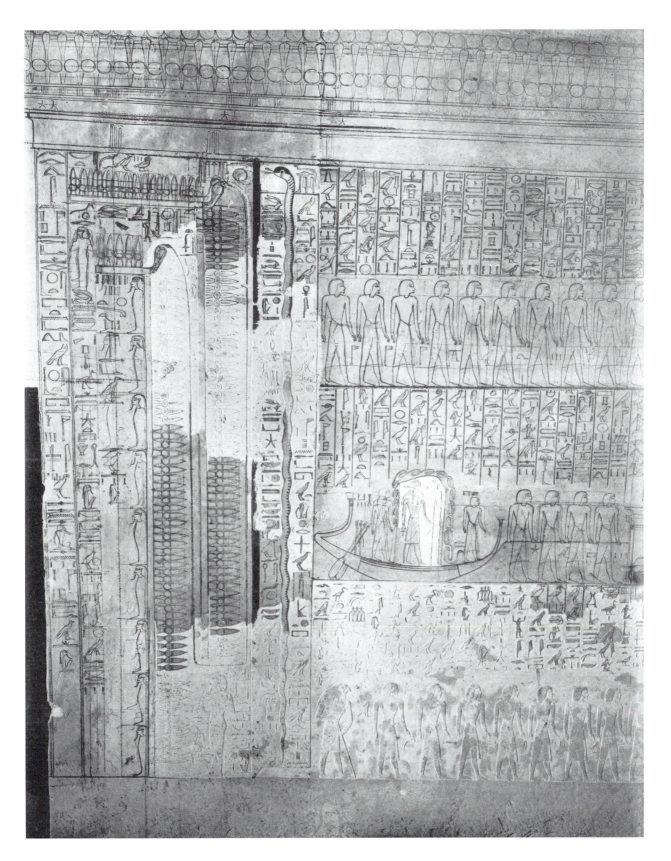

SOUTH PART OF WEST WALL FIRST SECTION.

PLATE XLVIII.

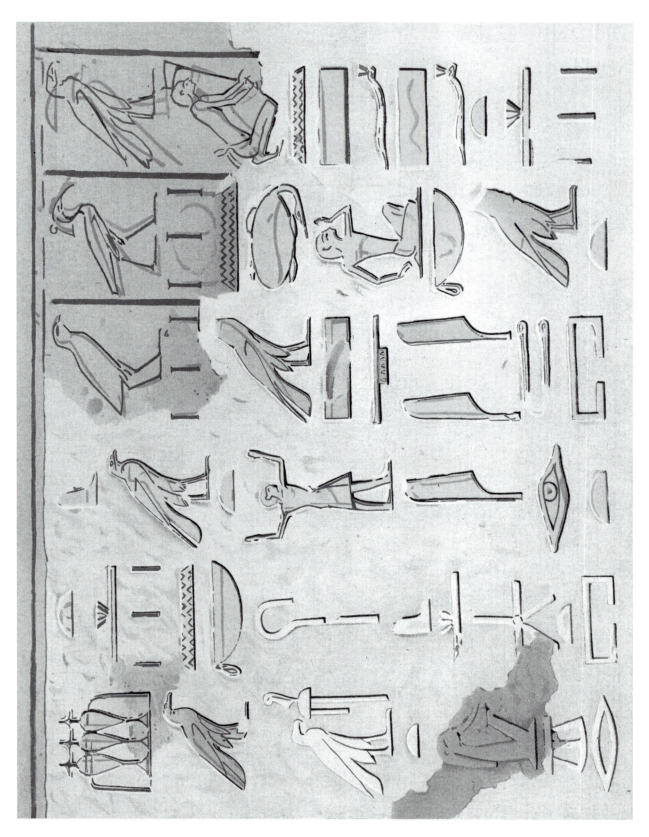

DETAILS OF HIEROGLYPHS FROM SOUTH PART OF WEST WALL

PLATE XLIX.

Golden Hall.

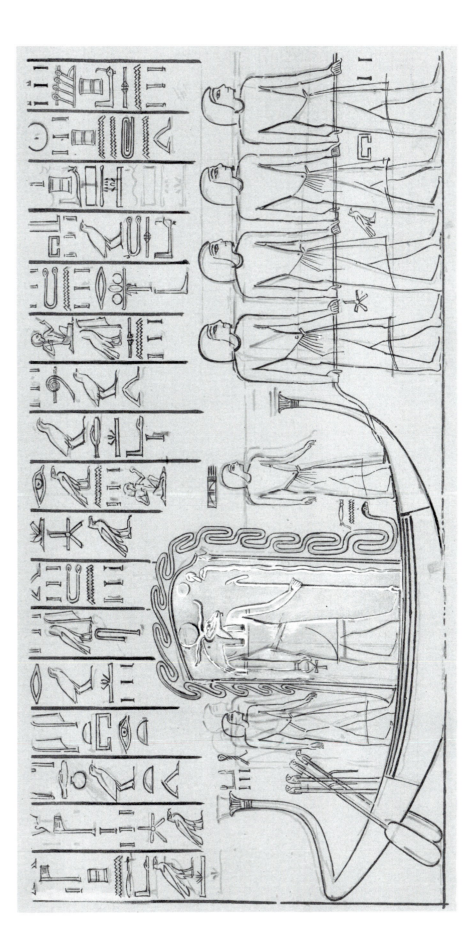

SOUTH PART OF WEST WALL: THE BOAT OF THE SUN

MIDDLE PART (1,) OF EAST WALL FIRST SECTION.

MIDDLE PART(2,) OF EAST WALL FIRST SECTION.

NORTH PART OF EAST WALL FIRST SECTION.

PLATE LXII.

ROOM BEHIND THE GOLDEN HALL.

DOOR OF THE LAST CELL.

THE FIGURE OF OSIRIS.

PLATE LXXV.

HEAD OF CANOPIC JAR.

PLATE LXXVI.

HEAD OF CANOPIC JAR.

PLATE LXXVII.

HEAD OF CANOPIC JAR.

PLATE LXXVIII.

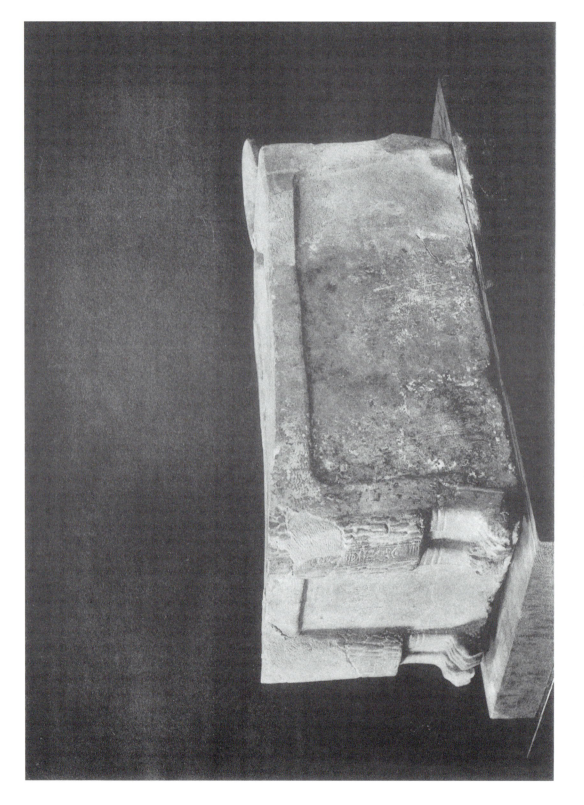

PLATE LXXIX.

ROYAL STATUE.

PLATE LXXX.

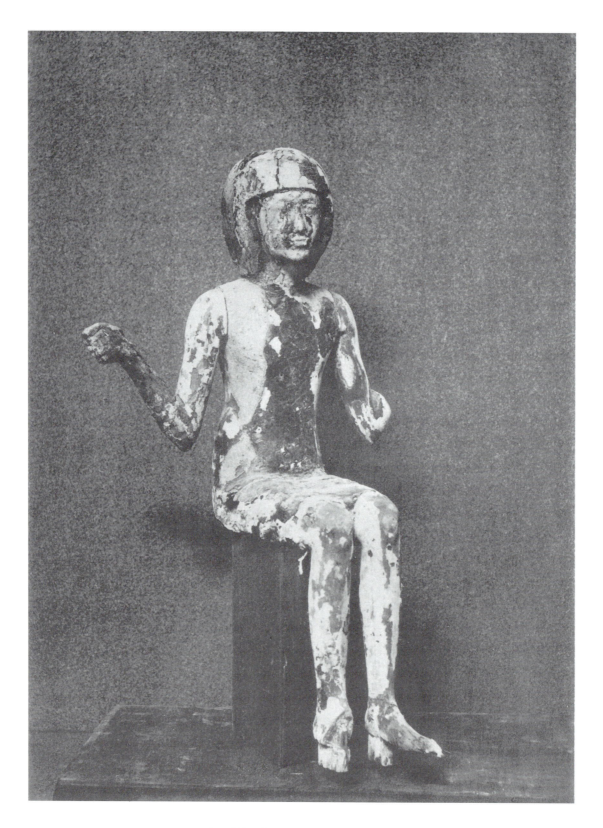

STATUE OF A SEATED GOD.

PLATE LXXXI.

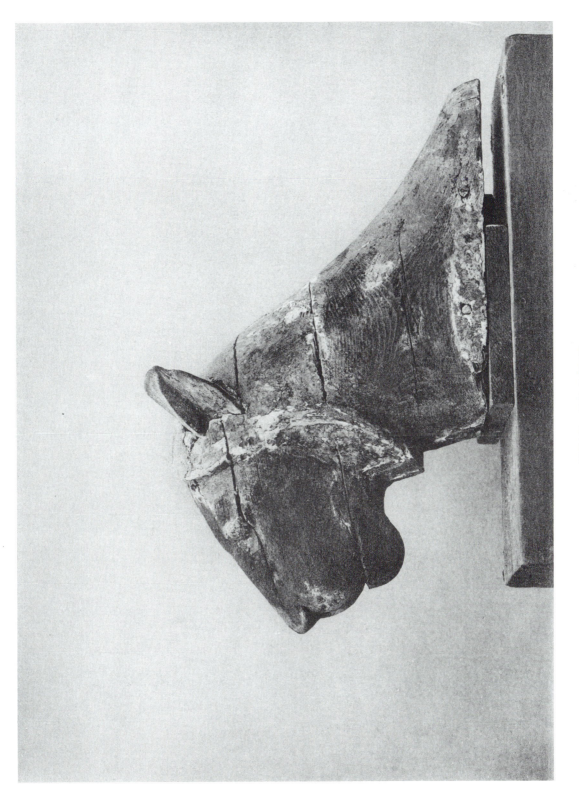

HEAD OF LION.

PLATE LXXXII.

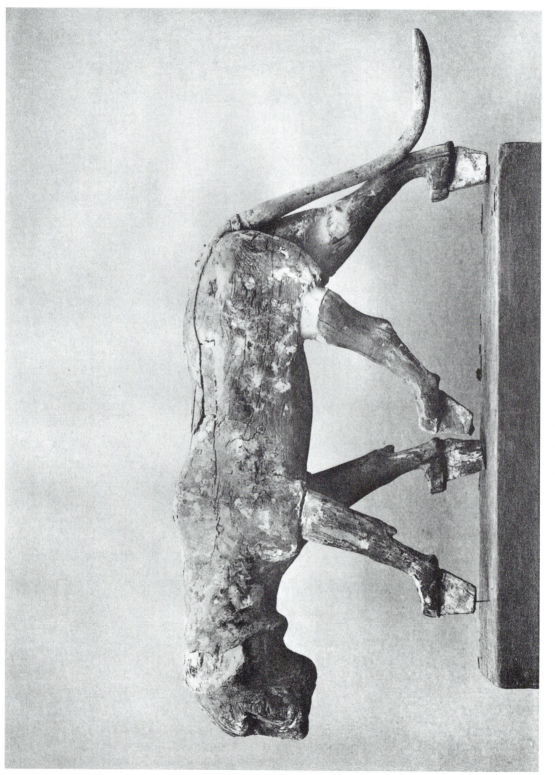

WOODEN PANTHER.

PLATE LXXXIII.

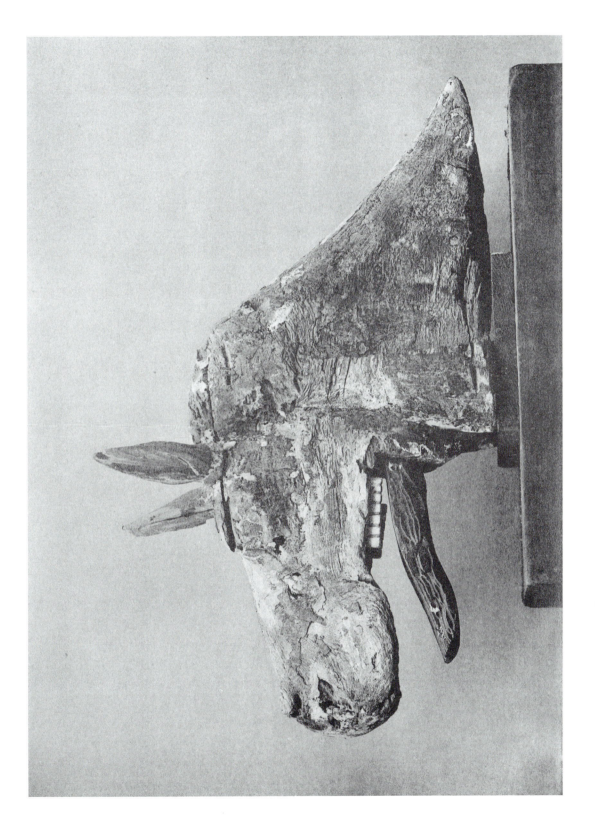

HIPPOPOTAMUS HEAD.

PLATE LXXXIV.

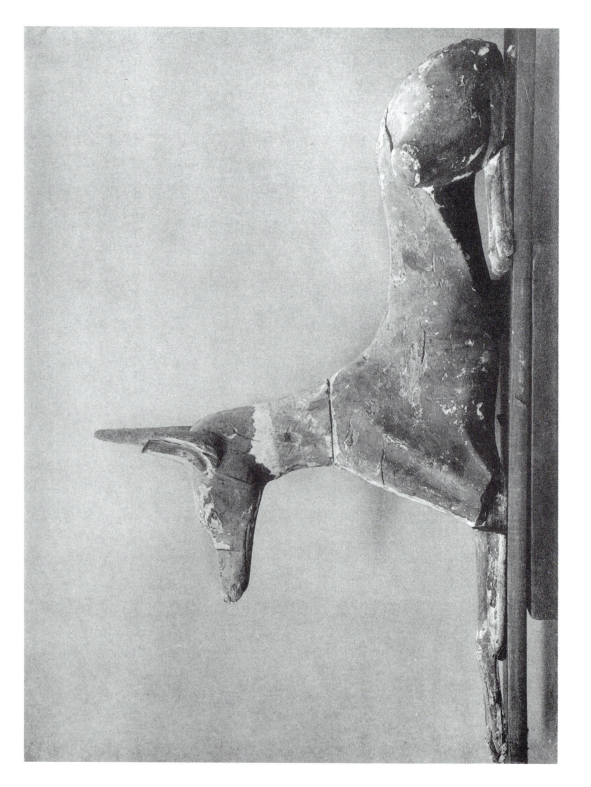

PLATE LXXXV.

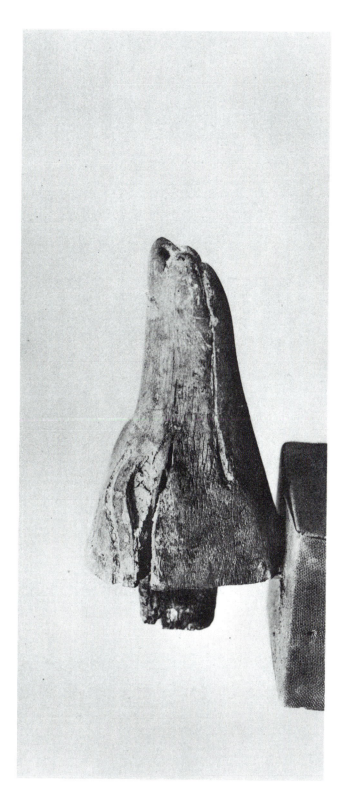

HEAD OF JACKAL.

PLATE LXXXVI.

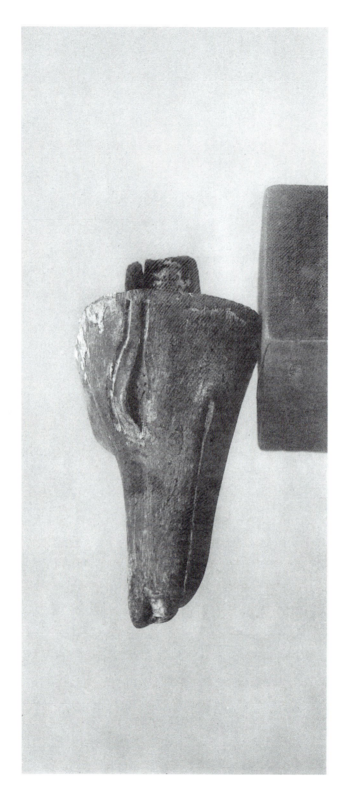

HEAD OF JACKAL.

PLATE LXXXVII.